And God Said…

An Absurd Tale of Love, Power, and Paperwork

Eric M. Ralph

DEDICATION

For my family.

ACKNOWLEDGEMENTS

Everyone who made this possible. My family. My readers – especially Leslie Hanzelka who read more than one draft, including the crazy draft.

APOLOGIA

I would like to sincerely apologize to anyone who might be offended by this book, including, but not limited to: Catholics, Christians, Jews, Scandinavians, Buddhists, homosexuals, homophobes, followers of Thor, Venus, or Odin, wrestlers, geographers, accountants, gun enthusiasts, gun control enthusiasts, Frank Herbert, Cinemax, David Lynch, Lou Ferrigno, Stanley Kubrick, Rod Stewart, Melissa Etheridge, the Partridge Family, Neil Diamond, Jimmy Buffet, Jimmy Carter, Buddy Holly, Spinal Tap, Galileo, Jamaicans, the people of Vatican City, Anglicans, whoever named Church House, idiots, John Carpenter, Ed Wood, Fred Astaire, fans of Dead Poets Society, farmers of green beans, drinkers of V8, Pat Sajak, Alex Trebek, and Bea Arthur. And Vanna White. With a special apology to Brian Ritchie. Truly, all is meant in good fun.

I steadfastly refuse to apologize to Sting or Michael Bolton. After all, they have yet to apologize to us.

CHAPTER ONE: GETTING YOUR BEARINGS

The sign outside read, "Giovanni's Italian Bistro: Serving the Nectar of the Gods 24 Hours a Day." Naturally, the sign didn't say that in most cases, the nectar of the gods was a good old Budweiser. Eli grabbed a towel and wiped down the dark mahogany bar. He looked out over the bright, airy dining room and out the glass doors to the boardwalk patio. The bar was busier than an average bar on Sunday nights. Eli's clientele didn't have jobs to go to, for the most part. The beginning of the work week hadn't meant anything to them when they were working gods and it meant even less now that they were retired. Owning the only Italian Bistro in Jamaica had turned out even better than he had expected. Having God on your side helped and having all the gods in history on your side was even better.

The Sunday tone was on the sedate side since the heavy partiers like Dionysus and Aegir were missing. More than likely they were still recovering from the previous night's festivities. The Sunday regulars tended to be the social drinkers, equally interested in drinking and talking. The conversation rarely turned confrontational, due to Eli's long-standing policy against discussing religion – including the secular version known as politics. Of course that left the most popular topic in play.

Eli drew a beer from the tap and handed it to the woman at the end of the bar. She attracted the attention of every male organism in the bar and rightly so. Venus was the most beautiful woman in history and a goddess to boot. Her rose-colored hair fell to her waist. Her cobalt blue dress exhibited her ample curves and accentuated her milky white skin.

Venus tipped Eli five dollars and turned her attention to the man seated next to her at the bar: A knight, complete in full armored regalia, sipping on a glass of what appeared to be a stout beer, but was, in fact, sarsaparilla.

"Hello," she said as she edged slightly closer to the knight. "I'm Venus."

She looked him up and down, her eyes flowing over his shining suit of armor, pausing for an extra second, perhaps, at the codpiece. A wily creature, Venus knew where a bit of extra attention would be appreciated.

Eli shook his head. That was the fifth different guy this week. Venus was such a tramp.

"I'm John," said the knight.

"Really, a knight," she said. "What do you do for fun?"

"I am on a great quest," said the knight, who was suddenly all too aware of his codpiece and trying desperately to keep his eyes at her neck or higher. Mostly he was failing.

"Really?" said Venus. "Tell me all about it."

John regarded her cautiously, but definitely not without interest. He didn't usually have extraordinarily beautiful women approaching him like this. He didn't want to be distracted from his quest, but a momentary dalliance might be quite enjoyable. For a moment.

"I am searching for the infamous Sampo," said the

knight. "A treasure beyond treasure, a jewel beyond jewels." He struggled to find the appropriate superlative. "A crème brûlée beyond crème brûlées."

Venus leaned forward in interest, accentuating her already profound chest, and put her hand on his knee briefly, expertly, before retreating.

"Sounds interesting. Where do you expect to find this Sampo of yours?"

"I know not where the Sampo may be found, but rest assured, I will find it. I will let nothing stand in my way," John paused dramatically, hoping Venus might express a bit more interest, lean a bit more his way, and maybe even reach out to touch him again. No luck. "I'm pretty sure, though, that it is around here somewhere. It's close, I can feel it. Practically taste it. The taste of victory."

"Ooh, sounds wonderful." Venus quivered temptingly in her chair.

"It is," said John, as he appreciated the quiet undulations before him.

"So you think it's right here in Vatican City?"

"Vatican City? I thought this was Kingston, Jamaica."

"It is," said Venus. "But the Vatican is right across the street."

She gestured out the window, where the Vatican stood in all its majesty, towering over the bar. St. Peter's Basilica, the Papal Palace, and St. Peter's square: It was all there. The Vatican, unmistakable, undeniable. Undeniably, unmistakably in Jamaica. John frowned at the Vatican, then turned back to Venus.

"That's a bit strange," said John. "I'm fairly certain the Vatican is supposed to be in Italy."

"Indeed."

John stood up and walked over to the window, allowing the Vatican to fill his field of vision. He stood entranced.

"So why is it here?"

Venus shrugged, her interest fading as the knight's

interest in her was displaced by a fascination with the Vatican, just meters away. Yards away, if you are American. John straightened, remembering his quest, and his eyes grew larger. Without a word, he left the bar. Behind him, Venus sighed and looked around the bar for her next conquest.

Her eyes rested on her next prospect, a nut she had tried to crack before, without success. He wasn't much to look at anymore. The years had caused his blonde hair to begin to turn prematurely gray and added stress lines around his blue eyes. He was still fairly fit, with just a hint of a potbelly beginning to emerge and still his arms and spine looked strong. His eyes were a bit tired, but his mouth remained ever young, mirthful. She hadn't seen him in years, but knew him immediately, despite the change in him. She slid into the empty seat at his table.

"God, I hope this seat isn't taken."

"Not at all. Nice to see you again, Venus."

"How long are you in town? We should catch up."

"I'd like to," he said. "But tonight's my last night. Vacation is over. I've got to go back home tomorrow."

"Well then," she said. "We'll just have to make tonight count, now won't we?"

Venus smiled and the man turned away and sighed. She picked up his drink and took a small sip. It was a Manhattan. Some things never change. She set the glass back down and slipped her hand onto his.

"Venus, I thought I had made myself clear the last time. I'm not interested."

"God, what's your problem? Don't you like me?"

"I like you fine," said God. "Just not interested in being another one of your conquests. Odin is right over there, though. He never seems to mind."

Venus took her hand away and leaned back in her chair. God gulped down the last of his drink and stood up. He bowed slightly and turned to leave. Venus sighed again, then looked over to where God had pointed. Sure enough,

Odin sat watching her. She thought he was winking at her. Since he had only one eye, she couldn't be sure. Either way, Odin was a sure thing and after two misses in a row, Venus needed a sure thing. She ambled over to his table and sat down. Odin smiled.

Outside God hailed a cab to head back to his hotel. He sighed as he settled into the backseat. He tended to become melancholy at the end of a vacation. He only took one week a year, usually in the spring, and always to Jamaica. He loved the Jamaicans. They always treated him very well and he loved their laid-back approach to life. He had a lot of followers in Jamaica, but they weren't too formal about it. God could go there and still cut loose a little bit, without it becoming a big thing. That just wouldn't work in, for example, Alabama. Not that anyone would ever vacation in Alabama anyway.

God's thoughts turned back to Venus. He did not regret brushing her off, but her advances, however unwelcome, did remind him of the gap in his life. While he enjoyed being god, it did have its downside. He didn't have any other active gods to turn to for support, encouragement, or even just simple empathy. Certainly there were no women to provide the comfort only a woman can. While God loved the Jamaicans and felt supported by them, it was not the same.

The joy God always felt when he arrived in Jamaica was always counterbalanced by the gloom that descended upon his return to New Jersey. He looked over Kingston from his hotel window as he got ready for bed and again sighed heavily. He smiled and gave the city a sad, silent goodbye. Reluctantly he shut the curtains, got into bed, and went to sleep. New Jersey awaited him in the morning.

CHAPTER TWO: YOUR FLIGHT HAS BEEN DELAYED

Sally felt her stomach tighten as the cab pulled up to the airport. She took a deep breath as she got out of the car, shifting from foot to foot as the driver retrieved her bags from the trunk. Once inside, she stood silent for a moment, in awe of the sheer size of the terminal. She sucked air, pausing just inside the entrance. The dinginess of the Newark airport passed unnoticed, since Sally had never seen any other airport to compare. After gathering her breath, she checked in and found the gate.

Sally sat down, clutching her purse and her package to her. She smoothed her jeans with her hands and fussed with the scrunchy holding in her loose ponytail. There weren't many people there yet since her flight wasn't due to depart for a couple of hours. She got out a magazine to read, but was too excited to concentrate. She wiggled in her seat as she waited, then got out her itinerary to review it for the umpteenth time. Her plan was to arrive in Los Angeles in time for dinner and get to bed early. That way she could get up in time to eat breakfast at her hotel before the show.

The gate started to buzz with people as the departure time crept nearer. Sally watched as businessmen spoke rapid-fire into cell phones while they struggled fruitlessly to connect their computers to the free WiFi. A man trudged by her and dumped his backpack in the seat across from her. He was no businessman. He wore blue jeans, classic Converse All-Stars, and a denim jacket. He rummaged through his pack until he zipped it shut with a deep sigh. He moved the bag to the floor, then dumped himself in its prior place on the seat. He pulled his hand through his blond hair, with flecks of gray starting to show, as he sighed again. He glanced up and his blue eyes met with Sally's brown.

"I forgot my book," he said.

"That's too bad. I'd offer you a magazine, but you don't look like a Cosmo reader."

"True," said the man, rubbing his chin, scratching at his two-day stubble. "I might get desperate, though. I was counting on my book to get me through the flight delay."

Sally craned her neck to look at the screens. The man looked involuntarily as the collar of her jacket pulled away, exposing the soft skin of her neck.

"What delay?" she said.

She turned back to the man, who made no effort to respond. Instead, he waited just a moment. The flight attendant's voice boomed over the public address system.

"Attention passengers flying to Los Angeles. Due to unfavorable weather in L.A., Flight 542 has been delayed two hours. We apologize for any inconvenience."

The man smiled and shrugged. The businessmen in the area groaned and chattered ever louder into their cell phones, frantically changing plans. Sally peered at the man with a wry smile.

"How did you know about the delay before anyone else?"

The man shrugged and adjusted his jacket.

"Lucky guess. Besides, with the track record of flights

to L.A., the smart money is always on a delay. Don't worry though. You'll make it in time for dinner."

He stretched his arms and leaned his head back, then cracked his knuckles.

"Arg," he said. "I hate California."

"So why are you going?"

"I'm going to the Lakers game tonight," he said.

"You're a Lakers fan?"

"Not exactly," he said. "More like a good luck charm. I help them win."

"How do you do that?"

"It's a long story."

The man rummaged in his pack again, his brow furrowed. He put a finger in the air and his eyes lit up. He flipped the backpack over and unzipped a small pocket hidden underneath a hand-sewn patch that read 'Trinity.' He fished out a small book, then smiled triumphantly. He opened the book and Sally couldn't help but glance at the title: *This Is Spinal Tap: The Book*. Sally had just returned to her magazine when she heard raised voices at the gate counter.

"What do you mean, I don't have a seat?" said an older lady, tucking her silver hair behind her ears. "I have a ticket."

"Yes," said the attendant. "But you don't have a boarding pass. You're flying standby and the flight is full. I'm afraid you aren't going to make it to Los Angeles today."

The woman's lips quivered and she ran her fingers through her hair. Sally strained to hear as the woman's voice softened.

"I'm sorry," said the woman. "But I really need to get to Los Angeles. Please. If there's anything you can do. My grandson is getting married. Please."

The woman's eyes pleaded with the gate agent. The agent bit his lip and eyed the screen in front of him. He shook his head.

"It doesn't look good. I'll do the best I can."

The woman forced a smile and nodded, then trudged over to her seat, just over Sally's shoulder. Sally turned to examine the video screens, which also turned her ear toward the woman, allowing Sally to hear the woman call her grandson.

"Yes, James," she said. "I know. I'm disappointed too. They are doing the best they can. We can only hope for the best. Either way, you have a lovely bride. I'm sure it will be a wonderful ceremony. I love you too. Bye bye."

A tear formed in Sally's eye and she turned to the man across from her.

"Isn't that terrible, she-"

Sally trailed off, discovering that she was talking to an abandoned backpack. The man was gone. She was just about to return to her magazine when she saw him walking back towards his seat. He nodded in greeting.

"I was just talking to you," said Sally. "I didn't realize you were gone."

"That's OK," said the man. "Just as long as I didn't answer you. I hate it when I have whole conversations while I'm away."

Sally chuckled and shook her head.

"No worries there. Just me talking to myself," she said. She pointed to the 'Trinity' patch on his backpack. "What's that?"

"Oh, that," said the man. "That's for my band: Trinity."

"Is that what you do for a living? You're a musician?"

"No, not really," said the man. "More of a side project."

"Why Trinity? Is Jesus on bass guitar?"

The man laughed.

"No, the Holy Ghost is on bass. Jesus plays lead."

Sally laughed again.

"So I guess that makes you God, the Father, on drums?"

"I'm the drummer all right," he said. "Most of the time, anyway. Sometimes we have another drummer play with us, so I can be out front. I'm the singer."

"Nice. Maybe I'll catch a show sometime."

"We mostly play in Jamaica," said God. "That's where the rest of the band lives. I vacation there whenever I can get away."

"That's too bad," said Sally. "I don't know many people around here, so I'm always looking for excuses to get out of the house."

"You live around here?"

"Yeah," she said. "In New York. I just moved from Iowa a few months ago."

God shook his head.

"You shouldn't have bothered. There's nothing in New York that Iowa doesn't have a better, less crowded, and cleaner version of."

"I'm not sure that it's Iowa you are thinking of," said Sally.

God shrugged. An attendant approached the microphone and spoke over the loudspeaker.

"Ms. Bonnie O'Hara, please check in at the counter."

Sally glimpsed the older woman in the corner of her eye. She rose slowly and tiptoed up to the counter. The woman's face lit up in astonishment as the attendant handed her a boarding pass. She could hardly keep her hand steady as she dialed her grandson to relay the good news.

Sally smiled as she turned back to God.

"That's great," said Sally. "I'm glad she made it on."

God nodded and leaned back in his seat. He glanced at the screen.

"Time flies," he said. "You'll be boarding soon, it looks like."

"Gosh, you're right," said Sally. "I can't believe it. I'm so excited. I've never flown before."

"Not even from Iowa to New York?"

"Nope. That was a road trip, all the way."

"Well, I hope you have a nice flight then."

Sally nodded as she gathered her things.

"Won't you be on the flight too?"

God shook his head and shifted in his seat.

"Nope. I'm on standby. It doesn't look like they'll have room for me. It's a full flight." God sighed. "No big deal. The Lakers will have to manage without me for a change. If they would just put in some effort on defense, they wouldn't need me anyway. Have a good trip."

Sally resisted the nearly automatic urge to say 'You too.' Instead she simply nodded again and rose with her purse in her hands, then wrestled her pack onto her shoulder. The attendant had her put her pack into the bin to make sure it would fit, and it barely squeezed into the allotted space. Sally stood awkwardly facing the gate, waiting for her seating priority to get called. She smiled at God, who smiled back. Finally her number was called. She waved shyly as she boarded the plane.

God waved back and sighed. He watched as Sally's plane taxied away from the gate, imagining her in her seat, the thrill she must have been feeling as the plane pulled away, accelerated, and then broke free of gravity and soared into the sky. He almost wished he were on the plane with her. He imagined being there, seeing her. Seeing everything with new eyes - her eyes, big, brown, and beautiful. He picked up his backpack and trudged down the hall, to the garage, to his car. He drove back to his home and his routine, trying not to think about the ebony beauty that had just boarded the plane.

On the plane, Sally smiled as she settled into her seat for the flight ahead. Her mind kept returning not to her flight, her trip to Hollywood, or Pat Sajak, but to the interesting, funny, and kind man she had just met in the airport. She had never even asked his name and yet she hoped she might somehow see him again.

CHAPTER THREE: GOD IS A WHEEL WATCHER

God went through his daily routine in a daze. He hadn't yet gotten back into the swing of things upon his return from vacation. Usually it took him about a week to get back in a groove, but it was already the end of week two, with no groove in sight. Whenever his mind wandered, it always went back to the airport, watching the plane depart. That shy wave as she boarded.

He did everything that he was supposed to do: Hearing prayers, inspiring athletes, and the like. He just didn't have any particular enthusiasm for it.

God answered some prayers half-heartedly, skimming them over before taking the necessary action. As a result of his inattention, he occasionally mixed up the prayers, with whimsical results. An Iowa middle-school teacher ended up scoring a game-winning touchdown while an NFL running back was graced with the sublime level of patience required to teach 8th-grade Spanish.

God decided to call it a day and make dinner. He gazed into the fridge, but nothing was really appealing. He went with a ham and cheese sandwich, mostly because anything else would have required more effort.

Still in a bad mood, God turned on the TV while he ate. Alex Trebek's self-satisfied expression filled the screen. God couldn't stand *Jeopardy!* Not only did God consider Alex insufferably smug, but he also couldn't stand the idiotic 'the-question-is-the-answer' conceit of the show.

God stormed back into the kitchen to get himself a good stiff drink. Unfortunately, Dionysus had dropped by the previous night and drank all the alcohol. The stiffest drink God had available was a V8 someone had brought for a party ages ago with vague intent of making Bloody Marys, but then Mary actually showed up and the whole idea became uncomfortable. His frustration building, God let out a scream and slammed the refrigerator door, causing small tremors in northern California.

"People think it's easy being God," he muttered to himself angrily. "They don't realize all the aggravations that go along with being the Almighty."

God paced up and down the kitchen floor, his steps resounding through the trailer, causing thunderstorms across the Midwest. He clenched his fist, then brought it swiftly down on the kitchen table, letting loose another yell. All across Michigan, people scurried inside, checking the weather alerts on their phones, and taking cover in their basements as storms thundered across the region.

God cleared his to-do list. He couldn't concentrate on the minor inconveniences of people's lives. They would have to fend for themselves for awhile. "Please God, help me, let me win the Lotto, please God, I've come down with male pattern baldness and the clap." How come no one calls just to say hi? God was sick of it.

He went into the living room to clean up his plate when he heard a familiar refrain. A crowd of people chanting in unison: "Wheel! Of! Fortune!" God liked *Wheel of Fortune.* It comforted him. The warm glow of the letters, the pleasant clicking of the wheel. He did miss the old shopping segment, where the contestants used to spend their winnings, but still he loved the show just the same. He forgot his worries for a moment and sat down to watch.

A familiar face was pondering her next selection. Her sable hair, no longer in a ponytail, fell over her petite, athletic frame. She tucked her hair behind her ear as she decided on a course of action.

"I'd like to buy an 'E'" said Sally.

"I'm sorry, but there aren't any 'E's," Pat said.

"What? That's not right. It's almost not an option to form a string of words without using a minimum count of that symbol," Sally said flatly.

"You seem to have just managed it," Pat said with a smug, Alex-Trebekian smile on his face.

"Oh, piss off!" the lady said.

The board behind Pat lit up with Sally's words.

"Congratulations," Pat said. "You've solved the puzzle!"

God paused the TV, with Sally filling the screen, captured in the moment of her victory. Her pearly-white teeth gleamed against her dark lips and her brown eyes twinkled with a light that perhaps none other than God would have seen. His features softened and his previous aggravation was forgotten. God was no longer bothered by the prayers, the ham sandwich, or even Alex Trebek. All of those things faded away, replaced by only - her.

God knew immediately what he needed to do. He had to find her. He wasn't going to wait around. He wasn't going to waste any time. He was going right to the top. God was going to call Pat Sajak.

CHAPTER FOUR: FRANK GETS THE CALL

Frank checked his watch and tapped his foot. It was almost noon. He could hardly wait for the bar to open and begin serving the free wine shots they had every Sunday. Ever since he had lost his job as bookkeeper for a world-renowned mad scientist, Frank had only his Sunday afternoon drinks to look forward to. There was something special about the wine; he couldn't help but take advantage whenever he could.

The bar opened and Frank got in line, with his secret flask hidden in his pocket. He had learned from bitter experience that the bartender hated it when people got in line more than once, so he planned to make the most of his one chance. He edged up to the server, took the vessel and faked a sneeze, turning away just long enough to empty it into his flask. He handed the vessel back, gave the bartender a thumbs-up, and made his way back to his seat.

Frank smiled. He had a good seat today - the first row. Last week he had gotten caught in the second row, behind some guy with the biggest hat Frank had ever seen. This week, the guy was sitting next to him and kept giving

Frank a weird look.

Frank ignored him. The singers were starting up and Frank jumped up to dance. He ran around like a maniac, looking for someone to mosh with, but the only other person in the pit was a funny-looking guy dressed in all black except for a white collar. Frank shrugged and slammed into him. The man in black signaled weakly as he fell to the ground and several men started converging on Frank.

'Uh oh,' Frank thought. 'Bouncers.'

The men grabbed Frank and threw him out the front door. The guy in the big hat came up and kicked Frank in the stomach while he was down. Frank lay on the ground, too tired to get up. The wine had hit him hard. Truth be told, Frank wasn't much of a drinker. To him, a V8 constituted a good stiff drink. Frank hated V8. He could feel rocks poking him as he lay on the ground, but couldn't bring himself to move.

Frank opened his eyes, hearing footsteps approaching. He saw eight legs in front of him, four male, four female. It took him a second to realize that they belonged to two different people. Frank was a little drunk. He grabbed hold of the man's legs and rested his head on the man's feet. The man jerked his foot away and Frank's head fell to the ground with a thud.

"What?" Frank heard the man say to the woman. "He was drooling on me."

The couple opened the door and went inside. Frank lay still on the ground like a slug. It was his only defense. Defense against what, Frank wasn't sure. I'm sure, but hey, I'm the omniscient narrator, so I know it all, but can't say anything. That would be telling. Besides, isn't it more fun to be kept in the dark for awhile?

Frank decided to crawl out of the way of the door. He really didn't want his head to be slammed into the pavement again. He crawled on all fours over to the wall and used it to get up. Frank took a labored breath and rubbed his forehead, concentrating on remaining upright. He was still leaning on the wall, but at least he was on two feet again. Frank decided to get out of there before the bar let out.

Frank went home and sat alone in a darkened room, the only light from the TV. The sound was turned low; he could barely even hear it. It didn't matter. He didn't care. Nothing mattered anymore. He had lost contact with all his former friends and family, even God seemed to have left him. Frank reached for the remote, struggling to move. His depression made even that simple motion difficult. Then the unexpected happened.

The doorbell rang.

Frank forced himself out of this seat and shuffled to the door. He opened the door to find a small dog looking at him with big blue eyes shining against his yellow-gray coat. The dog scampered through the door and jumped onto Frank's couch. Frank ambled after him, half-heartedly protesting.

"Hey," said Frank. "Get down from there. No dogs on the couch."

The dog looked at him, with its head cocked to one side, and said, "That's not a very enlightened attitude. Is this how you treat all your guests?"

It was then that Frank realized he was not talking with a talking dog, but with God. Frank always knew it was no coincidence that dog was god spelled backwards. This only confirmed his hypothesis.

"Hello, God," Frank said. "How have you been?"

"I could be better," God said, pawing at his nose. "I really wish Alex Trebek would wipe that smug smile off his face. Thinks he knows everything. I'd like to see him without those damn little cards with the answers on them and see how smart he is then."

Frank considered this for a moment. "Why are you here?"

"Aren't you expecting me?"

"No."

"Aren't you Pat Sajak?"

"No."

"Isn't this Tuesday?"

"No."

"Oh," God frowned. If you've never seen a dog frown, it's really kind of weird. "Terribly sorry to trouble you. And sorry about the mess."

And God left.

As Frank scrubbed the couch cushion, he tried to pinpoint exactly where his life had gone wrong. He thought about all the bad decisions he had made in his life. His decision to major in accounting. His decision to work as bookkeeper for a mad scientist bent on world domination. And finally, his decision to open the door for a small dog. Frank decided he was going to change his life. He was going to take control. He was going straight to the top. He was going to find God.

CHAPTER FIVE: THANK GOD FOR DVRS

God hung up the phone in disgust. After several calls, texts, and an in-person visit, God still couldn't locate Pat Sajak. God left a message with Pat's secretary, but he couldn't think of anything to say so he just told her to have Pat call his plumber as soon as possible. God figured, a plumber could always use extra work, so no harm was done.

God turned back to the TV, where Sally still smiled, frozen in time. He pushed 'Play' and watched the rest of the show. He absorbed every smile, every laugh, every twinkle in Sally's eyes. He toyed with his remote, fast-forwarding past the other contestants, replaying certain moments, and trying to pause at exactly the right instant. God went back and forth until he got it just right. His favorite moment was nothing exciting to the average viewer. The camera had lingered a moment on Sally before moving to the next contestant when her turn was over. In that brief moment, something inside Sally had changed. She had relaxed and in that moment, her true self had shown through. God thought it was beautiful.

God pressed 'Play' again and let the show finish. Sally made it to the bonus round and Pat introduced the puzzle category: Before and After. Sally scrutinized the puzzle closely as time ticked away. She bit the inside of her lip, concentrating on the glowing letters. God stared at the screen intently, urging her on as she hesitated. Her eyes brightened as she turned to Pat for a final guess.

"Is it: Jesus is love you long time?"

Pat paused dramatically, then broke into a broad smile. "That's correct!"

God clapped his hands and let out an involuntary yell. Sally's knees buckled, but she recovered quickly, eager to see what prize she had won. Pat held up the envelope she had selected before the bonus round. He focused intently as he opened it and removed the slip of paper within. He glanced at Sally as a sly grin crept across his face. Sally searched his face for any clue as to what the prize might be. She held her breath in anticipation.

"Congratulations, Sally. You have won a two-week, all-expenses paid, luxury vacation to Jamaica!"

Sally howled in excitement, not even hearing the announcer describe the trip she had won. She covered her face with her hands, sobbing with joy. The credits began to roll and God found that he had jumped out of his seat, pumping his fist with Sally's victory.

God composed himself and realized that he knew what he had to do. He had to pack. He was going to Jamaica.

CHAPTER SIX: DO NOT CALL AND ASK FOR CHUCK

Frank smiled. His quest was finally at an end. Since his brief, yet disturbing, encounter with God, Frank had a mission. Frank was going to find God.

Luckily, God had lost his collar as he had leapt onto Frank's couch. Frank inspected the collar and found God's address on the license. Frank now stood before Trailer 7, on Love and Rockets Drive in Florence, New Jersey. Frank was a little surprised. It looked like any other trailer in the park. No one would suspect who lived there. The only indication that God lived there was the mailbox, which said, of course, 'God' in clumsy, stick-on lettering.

Cautiously Frank knocked on the door. No answer. Frowning, Frank peered into a window, but it was too dark to see anything. Frustrated, Frank thought to himself, 'I knew I should have called ahead.' Frank was desperate. He backed up and took a running leap at the door, crashing into it at full speed. The door stood firm. Frank tried again. And again. And again. Exhausted, Frank leaned on the door, grabbing the knob for support. The knob turned under his weight and the door opened quietly.

Cursing himself silently, Frank entered God's trailer and looked around. Frank was struck by the total absence of anything in the trailer. Everywhere he looked, there was only nothing. Nothing, except for an answering machine lying in the middle of the floor. Frank walked up to it and pushed the button to hear the outgoing message.

"Hello, you have reached God's residence. I'm afraid I'm not in right now, as I have quit my job as God and moved to Jamaica. If you are interested in applying for the position of god, please leave your name and phone number after the beep. Thank you."

Frank cursed his luck and left the trailer, slamming the door behind him. This setback wasn't going to stop Frank. No way. Frank was going to Jamaica and Frank was going to find God, no matter what it took. Before that fateful night when God visited, Frank had lacked direction. No more. Frank was on a mission.

Inside the trailer, the answering machine played on, unheard by Frank.

"Hi, God, this is Chuck Niebaum. I understand that the position is now open and I'd like to apply. My number is 532-6184. Thanks."

CHAPTER SEVEN: NO CHARGE FOR PRETTY LADIES

Sally lay back in her seat after takeoff and slept during most of the flight to Jamaica. She was awakened with a start when the plane shook uncontrollably. Sally hurriedly removed the safety instruction booklet from the back of the seat in front of her, flipping through the packet, searching for the relevant information. Exasperated, Sally threw the packet away and decided on a new course of action: Panic. She grabbed her pack, strapped it to her back, leapt from her seat and elbowed her way past several elderly nuns with walkers suffering from multiple sclerosis (as if one sclerosis wasn't bad enough). She made it to the emergency exit, said a quick, silent prayer, and jumped. The parachute that people said she was crazy to bring ballooned open. Far above her in the plane, a flight attendant called out, "It's just turbulence!"

Sally landed safely on top of a jerk chicken stand. The corrugated roof clanged loudly as she walked to the edge and jumped to the ground. A small crowd of locals clapped appreciatively and Sally greeted them with a brief curtsey. The smell of the chicken hit her as she rid herself of the parachute. She hadn't eaten on the plane and the scent was unavoidable and irresistible.

"How much?" she said to the man at the grill.

"Nothing," said the man, smiling broadly with bright white teeth from underneath his battered canvas baseball cap. "No charge for pretty ladies that fall from the sky."

He handed her a bowl and she found a seat. She took a bite of the chicken, which tasted as good as it smelled. She savored the flavor, closing her eyes as the chicken slid down her throat. When she opened her eyes, a drink had appeared in front of her. Behind the drink was a familiar face, without the denim jacket.

"Oh my God," said Sally. "What are you doing here?"

"Buying you a drink," said God. "Rum is their specialty, you know. Best Mojitos in the world."

"But how did you find me?"

God shrugged and looked off to the side.

"Well," he said. "It was nothing really. I saw your show. You were great. I saw you won a trip here, so..."

"So you came to find me?"

God turned away again, his face flushed.

"It's too bad you didn't make the flight to Los Angeles with me," said Sally. "It would have saved you a lot of bother."

"That's true," God said. "But it's all for the best. I hate California. I try to keep people from moving there, but people seem to think that the nice weather is worth the earthquakes, floods, and forest fires. I really don't get that."

Sally looked confused. "How do you try to keep them from going? And why?"

"I just told you, with the earthquakes and all. And I hate California."

Sally looked even more confused, her head cocked to one side, her eyes narrowed.

"You talk as if you made the earthquakes and so on."

"That's right," God said cheerfully.

"How's that?" she asked.

"Well, I'm God," said God. "And you can do that type of thing when you're god. It's one of the perks."

"I see," Sally said slowly, humoring the man. "You're God."

"That's right."

"I thought you said you were in a band."

"I am in a band," said God. "Like I told you, that's just a side project."

Sally shook her head. "If you're God, then prove it."

God looked dumbfounded. "You want me to prove it to you?"

"Of course," Sally said. "Do you expect me just to buy something like that?"

"Well, yes," God said, scratching his head. "I've never been asked to prove it before, except by the occasional atheist, but no one really cares what they think anyway. Normally, I just say something like, 'You must have faith,' and people just kind of go, 'Oh, OK' and drop the whole thing."

"I see your point," Sally said slowly, not sure that either of them were making sense.

"So, just have faith," God said. "That makes everything much easier on both of us."

"Hmmm," Sally considered this carefully. "I guess so. OK."

God looked pleased. "Good. I was never good at the whole proof thing. Want to get some dessert?"

"Sure," Sally said. "Where should we go?"

"I know this great place just down the street."

"OK, let's go."

Sally and God chit-chatted as they walked down the street, until God turned into a building that looked like an Italian bistro. It was, in fact, an Italian bistro. The decor of the restaurant was normal enough, but the clientele surprised her. Just to her right was an Egyptian-looking man with the head of a hawk and sitting with him was a very petite woman wearing a horned hat and an animal pelt. The entire restaurant was filled with such characters and Sally looked around in wonder until a bolt of lightning broke her out of her awe.

"That idiot Thor," God said, as he gestured toward an impressively built man with blonde hair. "Always showing off, trying to pick a fight. Someday he's going to get kicked out of here. Then he'll be sorry."

"Thor?" Sally said, eyebrow raised.

"Yes, him, over there, with the big hammer. He's always causing trouble, a rabble-rouser, just like that damn squirrel Ratatoskr."

"Thor, like from the movies?"

"Don't let him hear you say that," God said. "He's the real thing, not some comic-book fantasy."

"Are all these other people gods too?" Sally asked.

"Oh no," God said, shaking his head. "Most of them are, but there's the occasional demon, or other spirit sometimes too, and sometimes a regular human, like you. They all come here to relax. Being a god isn't as easy as it looks you know."

"I can imagine," Sally said. She examined God's clothes again. They were pretty ragged.

"How is it that you can afford to eat here?" she inquired. "It's a pretty swanky place and frankly, you don't look like someone with a lot of cash. No offense."

God smiled. "None taken. Personally, I just point out where it says 'In God we trust' on the money and demand an unlimited credit line. For others, naturally, it's more difficult, since god is just their stature, not their name. Most others just put a penny or two in the bank and just wait until the interest is enough to pay the bill. Immortality does have its advantages."

As God and Sally ate their dessert and chatted over coffee, God's pager went off.

"Damn it," God said. "Sometimes I think this thing isn't worth the aggravation."

He looked at the pager, then looked around for the waiter to see where he could find a phone. The waiter was nowhere to be found.

"Why do you have a pager instead of a cell phone?" said Sally. "Who on earth has pagers anymore?"

"Don't start with that," said God. "I like my pager. With a cell phone, people feel like they have you at their beck and call. Don't answer someone's call, then they text you. Don't answer the text, they email you. Ignore the email and they call the rescue squad, since you must be dying in a ditch somewhere if they can't get ahold of you in thirty seconds or less. That was bad enough before I retired. With a pager, I can always tell people I got their page, but couldn't find a phone."

"But I'm surprised there are even still companies that offer pager service," said Sally. "Who's your provider?"

"The Shut-The-Hell-Up Pager Company, that's who," said God. He signaled the waiter to come over.

"Could you bring me a phone, please? I need to answer my page."

The waiter looked at God, looked at the pager, then looked back at God.

"Phone?"

"Yes, a phone," said God. "You punch numbers into it and another one rings somewhere until someone gets off the john and answers it? You know, a phone?"

"I don't know if we have one for guests to use," the waiter looked back toward the kitchen uncertainly.

"That's OK," said Sally. "Here, God, use my cell phone for crying out loud."

"Thanks," he said. "And sorry about the Shut-The-Hell-Up Pager Company remark. It's a sore subject."

God took the phone and looked at it.

"There aren't any buttons."

"It's a touchscreen."

God looked at her blankly.

"Here, let me."

Sally took the phone, dialed the number, and handed the phone back to God. God thanked her and put the phone to his ear.

"Hello, Chuck?" God said. "This is God. I understand you are interested in the position. I see. What do you think qualifies you to be god? Desire to dominate the world, I understand. Can you type? Yes, in English. Good. That will help with the paperwork. Yes, it is important. Well, I'd say you have the makings of a great god. Congratulations."

God hung up.

"Who was that?" Sally asked.

"Oh, that was the new guy. I just hired him to take my place."

"As god?"

"Of course," God replied. "I don't want to be god anymore. I decided to retire when I came down here to find you. It seems to be the place all the gods retire to. I thought it might be a sign to hang it up when you won your trip."

Sally considered. "So all these guys are retired?" she asked, gesturing around the restaurant.

"Naturally," God said. "They certainly wouldn't have time to eat here if they were still gods now would they?"

"I see your point," Sally admitted.

"Finished eating?" God asked.

"Yeah, sure."

"OK, let's go," God said as he rose from his seat.

Sally and God left the restaurant and took a walk down the beach. The sun was just setting, coloring the horizon an amazing mixture of colors, the red-orange of the sun contrasting with the deepening blue of the ocean. The pair walked in silence, the crash of the surf the only sound.

God was nervous, he wasn't sure how to act; he hadn't dated in centuries. Sure, he had success before, but Sally was very different from the girls God had seen before. That Mary Magdalene, for example, she was wild. Nothing like Sally. Sensing his apprehension, Sally took his arm.

God was inwardly pleased as they walked down the beach. "All right," he thought to himself. "I've still got it."

God slipped his arm around Sally's waist as they walked down the pier.

"You know," God said. "This is one thing I've never really understood."

"What's that?"

"Grape Nuts."

"Grape Nuts?"

"Yeah, you know. The cereal. It's one of the great mysteries of life."

Sally opened her mouth to protest, then shut it again, deciding it wasn't worth it. Then she opened it again.

"I thought god was supposed to know all the great mysteries of life," Sally said.

God sat up, looking intently at Sally.

"You know," God said. "That's one of the things that always annoyed me about the job. Everyone comes to me with their problems, asking the big questions, like 'Why am I here?' and so on, but no one ever stops to think that hey, maybe God is just as clueless as the rest of us. Maybe God is just some poor idiot that wouldn't know the answer to a deep question if it bit him on the ass."

Sally stared at him blankly.

"Not," God continued. "That I'm claiming that the answers to all the big questions are big, raving dogs or anything."

"Of course not," Sally said softly. "So, tell me about the new guy."

"Well," God said. "I don't know that much about him. It's not important, the job is really overrated. Nothing to it really. I think this guy was a mad scientist or something before, I'm not sure though. I just got the highlights of his experience. I didn't even read his resume. I just hope he can handle the incessant *Highway to Heaven* reruns. God I hate that show. Plus the paperwork. Mounds of it, every day, for any little thing. Very frustrating."

"Paperwork?"

"Yes, you know, forms to fill out, reports to submit. That type of thing."

"Submit to whom?"

"What do you mean, to whom?"

"Well," said Sally. "Someone must be asking you for the paperwork. Someone is looking at the reports you submit. Someone created those forms. Who ever told you to fill them out? Who created the forms in the first place?"

"I don't know. The gods before me told me I had to fill out these forms, so I filled them out. I never thought to question it. It's part of the job. When I took over they said, look, no matter what you do, don't forget to file your paperwork. And I never did."

"But why? Who told your predecessor to do it?"

"I'm sure he was told the same thing when he took the job. Even Trall complained about the paperwork, for crying out loud."

"Who is Trall?"

"Trall is the oldest god I know. He was god ten thousand years ago or something like that. He had it rough, lived in a cave most of his reign. He's not too pretty to look at either. He's not entirely human. A kind of a mix between human, bullfrog, bat, and who knows what."

"Didn't you ever wonder about the reason behind it all?"

God smiled and took Sally by the hand. Overhead seagulls called and in the back of his mind, God worried about a potential dropping situation.

"If there's one thing I've learned over the years," God said. "It's that not everything has a reason behind it."

"I understand," said Sally, though she wasn't sure she did.

"Besides, Trall said that once he was late submitting his paperwork and then in no time the dinosaurs were wiped out."

"What?" said Sally. "What happened?"

"Trall was a little vague on the details. A lot of fire, brimstone, that type of thing. I didn't press him on it. You never wanted to spend any extra time with Trall. The smell is unimaginable. That's what he said though. I'm not sure if it is true. No sense taking a risk on something like that."

"That makes sense," said Sally. "I guess I understand."

"Good," God said. "That's two, if you're scoring at home, or even if you're by yourself."

"Two what?" Sally asked, confused.

"I don't know," God said as he rubbed his chin. "Never thought about it. I just love those guys on SportsCenter that used to say that."

"Wasn't that like twenty years ago?"

"So?"

"So you're still using it?"

"It's still funny, even though it's twenty years later. People still use 'scoring' to mean sex, right?"

"I suppose, but still."

"What is it with you?" said God. "This is our first date and you're acting like my wife already."

"That's a weird thing to say, why do you assume a wife always gives her husband a hard time?"

"Thousands of years of human history," said God.

CHAPTER EIGHT: FENRIR, THE WOLF

Frank strode through the Jamaican airport. It had been quite a flight. The Pope had also been on the flight and Frank had gotten to sit next to him through a computer mix up that put Frank next to the Pope in first class while a Cardinal had to sit next to an old crotchety guy that suffered from severe digestive problems back in coach. The trip was fairly enjoyable; the only thing that bothered Frank was that the Pope had continually referred to Frank as Tito. Whenever Frank would try to tell him that his name wasn't Tito, the Pope would get pretty mad and point to his hat, saying, "See the hat? That means I'm the Pope and I just suppose you've never heard of papal infallibility? It extends to the papal airline, you know. The airline computer says you are Tito, so you're Tito. End of story." Finally, Frank let the subject drop.

"You know," Frank said to the Pope. "I really expected you to be taller."

Making sure to get a picture of himself with the Pope before he left, Frank was now prepared to continue his search for God. With his genuine Pope hat signed by the Pope himself (*Dear Tito, you were always my favorite of the five, sincerely, Pope John Paul Georgianringo*), Frank hailed a taxi and

32

rode to the beach. He checked into a hotel on the boardwalk and went to sleep for the night, intending to begin his search fresh in the morning.

Frank got up the next morning, feeling invigorated after a good night's sleep. He wasn't sure where to look for God. He decided he would snag some breakfast and ask around to see if anyone had seen God lately. He left the hotel and walked down to an Italian bistro he had seen down the boardwalk.

Frank went into the bistro and sat down at the bar. He looked around and thought to himself that Jamaicans looked a little different than he had expected.

"What a bunch of freaks," Frank muttered to himself as he eyed the impressively built Jamaican wearing a horned hat and carrying an extremely large hammer.

"What did you say?" the man said, shaking his hammer in Frank's face.

Frank shrank in his seat. The man was twice his size and was all muscle. Frank, on the other hand, was a sizable man, but with a much more spongelike consistency.

"Uh, nothing," Frank said, smiling nervously. "Nothing at all."

"It had better be, otherwise I'd feed you to Fenrir."

"And none of us want that."

"What?"

"I said none of us want that."

"Are you making fun of me?"

"No," Frank said. "Of course not, I would never, ever, even think of, uh…"

"Good," the man sat down next to him. "Barkeep! Get my little friend here a drink."

"Oh, no," Frank said as the bartender poured the drink. "That's really not necessary. It's awfully early."

"You refuse the hospitality of Thor?" The man said.

"Why no," Frank said. "It's just that, uh…Well, I guess just one couldn't hurt."

Frank took a sip of the drink.

"Ulraaarg," said Frank. Thor laughed.

"Down it all," said Thor. "That's the only way to do it. Like this: To victory and power!"

Thor downed the drink with a flourish and slammed the glass onto the bar. Frank smiled weakly, raised the glass to his lips, and finished the drink in one gulp.

"Ulaulararrrgulaulararrrg!" said Frank.

Thor laughed again.

"Nicely done, little man," said Thor.

Frank smiled weakly and fell out of his chair. Lucky for him, he was already too drunk to notice. He turned to Thor's foot and explained that he was here to find God. Thor's foot was unimpressed. Frank fell back and passed out on the restaurant floor, just as the door opened, and God and Sally walked in.

"Another friend, Thor?" asked God, gesturing to Frank's prone form.

Thor nodded.

"This one didn't even make it past one."

God laughed and guided Sally to a table by the window.

Sally and God had an enjoyable breakfast, watching the sun rise through the window as they ate. God turned away, while Sally was entranced.

"What's the matter?" Sally asked. "The sun rise is beautiful."

"Eh," God said noncommittally. "Seen it too many times before, I guess."

Sally reached across the table and took God's hand.

"It's the first time with me."

God looked up and thought, 'Wow, I got a live one here.'

"I guess you're right," he said, appreciating the sunrise as if new. Just as he was starting to enjoy it, he felt a hand grope his ankle. God looked down to see Frank holding his foot.

"Hey," Frank said drunkenly. "You seen God lately?"

"As a matter of fact, I have," God answered. "You're

looking at him."

God's words fell on deaf ears. Or more correctly, passed out ears. Frank was out again, a small pool of drool collecting on God's shoes. God jerked his foot away reflexively and Frank's head fell with a thud. Sally looked at God, who shrugged.

"What can I say?" God said. "He was drooling on me."

CHAPTER NINE: SOMETIMES WHEN YOU NEED A DUNGEON, YOU HAVE TO IMPROVISE

Sunday services at the Vatican were always a special event. The majesty of St. Peter's granted the services a dignity and honor that cannot compare to any other facility. Nothing could spoil the experience for a dedicated Catholic. Not even the Pope kicking a man in the ribs in the middle of Sunday services.

This wasn't usual practice at the Vatican, but this poor sap deserved it. If there was anything that annoyed the Pope, it was moshing (while drunk) during a sermon. It simply isn't done. At least, not in the Vatican. Sure, the Unitarians could have their fun in their own churches, but not when the Pope was running the show. The Vatican bouncers came and dumped the unfortunate young man outside the door.

"Go have a V8!" the Pope yelled after the drunken idiot. He fumed through mass, then stomped into his office to try to address a seemingly intractable problem facing the Church. The Pope loved V8, but he hated green beans. This was not the Pope's biggest problem. The

Pope's biggest problem as he saw it was the break-up of the Jackson Five. The Pope's biggest problem as virtually everyone else saw it was the Anglican Church. However, a third problem presently held the Pope's attention. The problem was a simple one. Bubble gum.

A casual observer would not expect bubble gum to be a prime concern of the papacy. That's why those kinds of observers are called 'casual,' the term 'casual' in this sense meaning 'wrong.' In reality, bubble gum worried the Pope more than anything else – other than the Jackson Five. Or more precisely, the Pope worried that he would be stuck with the extraordinarily massive amount of bubble gum he had purchased from Joe Mahmuh to sell in the Vatican's annual fundraiser. The Pope had briefly considered replacing the Communion Wafer with Communion Bubble Gum, but decided against it on the basis that it would bring too many kids to Mass and god did he hate it when they started screaming right in the middle of the Lord's Prayer.

The Pope continued to worry until Cardinal Tito interrupted his worrying with some good news.

"Sir," Tito said. "I have some good news."

"Eh?" the Pope said. "What is it then? Are the Jackson Five getting back together?"

Tito grimaced. "I'm afraid not, sir. It's Joe Mahmuh. We've found him."

The Pope smiled. "Good. Put him in the dungeon and feed him only green beans."

"Sir?"

"What?" the Pope said.

"The Vatican doesn't have a dungeon."

"Then put him in one of the bedrooms and call it a dungeon. He won't know the difference. How many dungeons has the average person ever seen? None, so he won't have any idea it isn't a dungeon unless you tell him. Jesus Christ, do I have to think of everything myself?"

Tito nodded and left without a word. The Pope sat

back in his giant leather desk chair, enjoying the moment. His agents had finally captured the elusive Joe Mahmuh, the man who had stuck him with more than two million pieces of bubble gum. Well, the Pope would soon teach Joe Mahmuh about the negative side effects of overly aggressive marketing tactics. The Spanish Inquisition would pale by comparison.

CHAPTER TEN: GOD GETS A CATCHPHRASE

Sally and God had just finished dinner. God's apartment was sparsely furnished and had not yet acquired the 'lived-in' quality that comes only with time. They adjourned to the living room, where the fireplace glowed with the inviting crackle of fire. They watched the sun slowly disappear over the horizon as they sat in each other's arms. The glow of the candles flickered noiselessly. God smiled nervously as he placed his hand in hers.

"Sally?"

"Yes, God?"

"Sally, I've got something to say, but I'm afraid."

"Don't be. It's all right."

"OK," God said. "Here goes."

God rose form the couch, then got down on one knee beside Sally.

"I've been waiting," God sang. "For a girl like you to come and be my wife. Waiting for someone new, whose love I will survive…"

"God," Sally said. "Please stop that."

"What?" God said. "I'm trying to be romantic."

"OK, problem number one: Foreigner songs haven't been considered romantic since 1987. If then. Problem number two: Those aren't even the right words. I'm sorry."

"Well then," God said. "Excuse me for trying to express my feelings."

"I said I'm sorry," Sally said. "Go on, express your feelings. Just use your own words, not Lou Gramm's."

"Lou Gramm?" said God. "I thought it was Lou Rawls."

"That's so wrong, I don't even know where to begin."

"Sorry," said God. "I guess it's not important."

"No, it's not important," said Sally. "So you were saying?"

"I really don't remember now," said God. "The whole Lou Gramm-Lou Rawls thing really threw me for a loop. One of those things that makes you question everything you think you know. Kind of like when I found out that Kyle MacLachlan doesn't like cherry pie. What's his problem anyway? What's not to like? It's sweet, a little bit tart - it's delicious!"

"God, you're losing focus. Something made you sing that Foreigner song and I want to know what it was."

"OK, OK," said God. "Whew."

God rubbed his forehead, then flailed his arms around, stretching them out. He jumped up, shook his whole body, then started circling his head around like a madman.

"What are you doing?" said Sally. "Stop it right now."

"Sorry, sorry," said God again. "Just trying to relax, you know, loosen up a bit."

God took a deep breath and knelt before Sally once again.

"What I'm trying to say is," said God. "I love you more than Swedish fish - the red kind. To me you're like the movie *Big*. Sweet, funny, lovable, and sexy as long as you don't think too hard about it really being a thirty-something woman getting it on with a pre-teen. If you marry me, I promise I'll do my best to make our marriage like *The Greatest American Hero* - still the best thing on TV thirty years later. Will you be my wife?"

"Of course!" said Sally.

God took out a gigantic ring and slid it on her finger. Sally kissed him and then squeezed him tightly. God was happier than he had been since he figured out how he could make a rock so heavy even he couldn't lift it.

"Now I'm driving the bus!" said God.

"What?" said Sally.

"I said, 'Now I'm driving the bus!" God said. "It's my new catchphrase."

"Catchphrase?"

"Yeah," said God. "You know, something that when people hear it, or read it in the paper, they think of me."

"Don't you think you have that already?" said Sally. "There are lots of things in the Bible everyone knows, like 'Thou Shalt Not Kill.'"

"Sure, there is that," said God. "Nothing against the Bible, but that's not a catchphrase. It's kind of hard to drop 'Thou Shalt Not Kill' into casual conversation."

"OK, fine, you're right," said Sally. "What's this catchphrase again?"

"OK, are you ready this time?" said God. He paused dramatically, as if he were trying to solve a calculus problem in his head in time to convince a computer of the futility of nuclear war. "Here it is: Now I'm driving the bus."

"Now I'm driving – the bus?" said Sally. "How's that supposed to be dropped into casual conversation? Excluding conversations between bus drivers?"

"Well, it's not that you're literally driving the bus. It's metaphorical. It means you've got it going on, you're in control, you're with it. Who's driving the bus? You are!"

"Wait a minute," said Sally. "Am I driving the bus, or are you driving the bus?"

"Right now, no one's driving the bus. But if you were

really with it, I could say, 'Now Sally's driving the bus!'"

"So I'm not with it right now?"

"Uh, OK, that wasn't a good example. If anyone's driving the bus, it's you," said God. "Not me. I'm not driving the bus. If anything, I'm, uh, under it."

Sally smiled. "Oh, it's OK, I know you didn't mean it that way. You can drive my bus any time."

Sally kissed him.

"Thank me," said God. "I was worried there for a second." God shuffled his feet and glanced back at Sally. "By driving your bus, you meant sex, right?"

"Of course," said Sally.

"Good," said God. "I wasn't sure I'd be comfortable being engaged to a woman who owned her own bus."

CHAPTER ELEVEN: NOBODY
EXPECTS THE SPANISH INQUISITION

Joe Mahmuh was hungry for a big, juicy steak. He had been a prisoner of the Vatican for nearly a week and since his capture he had eaten nothing but green beans, by direct order of the Pope. Joe liked green beans, but it was a little much having them three times a day. Otherwise Joe was fine. The dungeon was actually a rather spacious bedroom suite. A huge four-post bed sat on an elevated platform in the middle of the room, while in the living area one wall was filled with high-end electronics. There were French doors that opened onto a balcony overlooking the entire city. A plaque on the wall claimed the Queen of England herself had once stayed there. Joe was lounging on the balcony, watching the traffic flow by when he heard a knock at the door. The Pope walked in and greeted Joe with a smile.

"Hello, Joe," the Pope said. "Or do you prefer to be called Mr. Mahmuh?"

"Joe's fine," said Joe. "What are you doing here?"

"I came to give you a treat," the Pope said. "Here you are."

The Pope handed Joe a V8. Joe hated V8.

"Uh, thanks," Joe said. "I think I'll save it for later."

Joe set the V8 down on the coffee table and made a mental note to flush it down the toilet later.

"So," the Pope said, smiling. "How's the food?"

"Really good, actually," Joe said. "I love green beans and you have an excellent chef. I feel like I've been the judge on the green bean episode of Iron Chef America."

The Pope scowled. "Oh well. Have you had time to think about what you've done?"

"What do you mean?" Joe said.

"About the two million pieces of bubble gum we couldn't sell like you said we could. It wasn't a fundraiser. It was a fundlowerer."

"Oh, that," Joe said. "Carpe Diem. That's all I can say."

"'Seize the day'?" the Pope said. "What the hell is that supposed to mean? You're not going to stand on a desk now, are you?"

"Oh, no. Not Carpe Diem," Joe said, tapping his toe impatiently and snapping his fingers, as if that would help him come up with the right term instead of just making him seem like the most rhythmless person east of the Mississippi, which, coincidentally, he was. "Damn. I mean Caveat Emptor. Buyer beware."

The Pope fumed. "Look," he said. "I have two million pieces of bubble gum and nothing to do with them. You'd better help me out, or else."

"Or else what?" Joe said. "You're Catholic and all the good tortures are sins."

The Pope paused. Joe had a point. The Bible, while all well and good most of the time, could put a damper on things when torture was involved.

"Well," the Pope said. "If other Popes can send kids on Crusades, lead the Spanish Inquisition, and approve of Jimmy Carter as President, I think torturing a bubble-gum sales representative would be permissible."

Joe was at a loss. "OK, you have a point," he said. "But

I'm impervious to most methods of torture any humane being would use."

"That's fine," the Pope said. "Shall we get started?"

The Pope beckoned to Cardinal Tito, who was waiting outside the door. Cardinal Tito poked his head inside.

"Now?" said Tito.

"Now," said the Pope. Tito disappeared as the Pope followed behind him. Joe detected a gleam in the Pope's eye as he paused briefly at the door before closing and locking it behind him. Joe turned as the wall of electronics clicked alive, a wall of lights running up and down then stopping. A moment of silence. The wall erupted with music, a bit louder than Joe would like, but not dangerously so. He inspected the equipment closely, but none of the controls seemed to work. He shrugged, then sat down to relax.

The music rose, the instrumental now interrupted by a distinctive tenor voice.

"Oh no."

Joe sat up and approached the wall of electronics with new resolve. The tenor voice grew louder into the chorus. *How Am I Supposed to Live Without You...* Joe frantically twisted the knobs in hopes that one of them would, if not silence the music, switch it to something less grating. Nothing changed.

Joe switched tactics and looked around for anything he could use to destroy the stereo system. The throw pillows and cushions taunted him; there was nothing he could use. He reared back and kicked at the stereo, but it would not stop: Bolton howled through the chorus, bringing Joe to his knees, his hands to his ears. He rushed to the balcony, but the doors had somehow been closed and locked.

Joe ran to the bed and tried in vain to block the sound from his ears with a set of pillows. He curled into the fetal position and began shouting to fill his ears with something besides Michael Bolton. After four minutes and fourteen seconds, Joe stopped shouting. The stereo had gone silent.

After one blissful, sweet moment of silence, the stereo began to again reverberate with music. When Joe heard the familiar first strains of an Otis Redding classic, somehow Joe knew that the song was not going to be sung by Otis Redding. Joe again fell to his knees, no longer yelling, but sobbing. He pounded his fists on the floor.

"No," Joe moaned. "That's it. I give up. Whatever you want. Just stop. For the love of God, stop."

The music paused and the Pope's voice boomed over the system.

"Perhaps this ugliness could be avoided," the Pope said. "If a refund could be issued?"

"Fine. Fine. Anything," Joe said. "Just don't play that ever again."

The Pope entered the room with a broad smile. He rubbed his hands together as Joe pulled himself together. He got out his checkbook.

"Do you have your receipt?"

"Yes," the Pope said. "Let me find it." The Pope began to search through his robes for his wallet. Joe heard a shout from the street and strode to the balcony, the doors now unlocked, to see what it was. The Pope followed close behind. They saw a man dressed in armor hailing them from the street.

"Hey there," the man shouted. "Either of you two seen a Sampo anywhere?"

"No," Joe said.

"No," the Pope said.

"Damn," the man said as he hurried off.

"What was that about?" Joe asked.

"I don't care," the Pope said as he dug into his wallet. "Here's the receipt."

"Thanks," Joe said as he returned the Pope's money. "Sure are a lot of freaks running around the Vatican."

The Pope looked around. "What do you mean? Is Madonna here?"

"No," Joe Mahmuh said. "Forget it. Never mind. Can I

go now?"

"Huh? Oh, of course," said the Pope.

The Pope smiled and turned on the TV, relaxing in the glory of his victory over the bubblegum salesman. He felt on top of the world. He didn't think there was anything that could make him feel better than he did at this moment.

The Pope's cell phone rang and the Pope answered.

"Hello?"

"Hello, is this Pope John Paul Georgianringo?"

"Yes. How can I help you?"

"You suck. You're the worst Pope since that time when they had, like, five Popes running around Europe all at once."

"Who is this?"

"You don't know me," said the caller. "You think you're so great, with your big hat. Why's you're hat so big anyway, big hat? Seems like you're compensating for something."

The Pope frowned, trying to figure out who would call to insult him like this.

"Carl? Carl, is that you?"

"Uh, no. Like I said, you don't know me."

The Pope looked at the phone, where the caller ID listed the main phone number of the Church of England.

"It is you. Carl, you're the Archbishop of Canterbury for crying out loud. Show some dignity."

"You show some dignity," said the Archbishop.

"I'm hanging up now. Maybe the Church of England would be taken a little more seriously if you would just grow up a little."

"That's rich coming from you. Hey look! It's Michael Jackson!"

The Pope hung up and shook his head. The Archbishop would have to learn a lesson someday. Maybe that lesson would just be not to make prank calls from office lines, but a lesson would be learned. Someday.

CHAPTER TWELVE: THE REAL REASON BEHIND PLUTO

"What's wrong with people?" said God as he read over the morning paper. "I don't know everything, but I know some things, which is more than I can say for most people."

God sat across the kitchen table from Sally, who was eating a breakfast of bacon and eggs. God had surprised Sally by cooking breakfast and doing it pretty well. The bacon was just the right crispness and the eggs were soft, light, and fluffy. Sally sat cross-legged on the chair, still dressed in her flannel pajamas. Already God's apartment felt just a bit like home.

"Yeah," said Sally. "I know what you mean, people can be really – wait a minute. You're God. You do know everything."

God put the newspaper down and paused for a second.

"Well," said God, glancing quickly from side to side. "Not exactly."

"What does that mean?"

"You see, it's like this," God said. "I don't really know everything. But I can look stuff up."

"So you just look everything up?"

"Yeah, I guess you could say that," said God, shifting his weight in his chair. "More or less. I mean, I can look up whatever anyone else can look up. If I can't look it up, neither can anyone else, so who's the wiser? Maybe I don't look up every single little fact, but basically yeah, I look stuff up."

God inspected the plate of bacon, took a piece that met his standards, and popped it in his mouth. He looked up to see Sally staring straight at him.

"You don't look anything up, do you?" she said.

God turned his palms to the ceiling and gave a half-hearted shrug. "What do you mean I don't look anything up? I just said I did, sort of." He glanced from side to side. "OK, so maybe I don't really look up every minute detail. But I always answer people's questions."

"So if you don't know, you just make it up?"

"I wouldn't say it that way. I make educated guesses."

"Based on?"

"Based on, uh, the um, nothimim."

"Come again? You didn't say anything, you just kind of trailed off."

"Yeah, I guess I did kind of, uh, trail off…"

"So your 'educated guesses' are based on…?"

God clasped his hands and flicked the nail on his left thumb with his right pinkie.

"Uh, nothing."

"Nothing?" Sally's eyes fell.

"Right," said God. "And since I'm God, no one checks on me afterward."

"You're OK with that?"

"Sure, sure," said God. "Though I feel bad about Galileo." God stretched out his arm, examining his fingernails.

"Galileo?"

"Yeah," he said. "You know Galileo. He asked me once about whether the earth was the center of the universe or not. I told him it wasn't, without looking it up first. As it turns out, it was."

"The Earth is not the center of the universe," said Sally.

"Not anymore," said God. "I changed it later to make it up to him."

"Changed what later?"

"Everything," said God, throwing his hands up. "You know, the universe. The whole shebang. Switched everything around. It took forever. Never did like where Pluto ended up. Kind of hanging out there on the edge of the solar system. But it was the best I could do."

"I think it worked out fine," said Sally.

"Tell that to Galileo. You weren't fed to alligators, or lions, or whatever they did to him. I've never had a mind for detail," God glanced up at her. "Of course, I could look it up…"

"Don't bother with that right now," said Sally. "Galileo can wait. We've got a wedding to plan."

Sally got up from her seat and poured herself a fresh cup of coffee. She took in the aroma before taking a drink.

"Where should we have the ceremony?" she said.

God shrugged. "I don't know. Can't you just decide everything? Just let me know when and where to show up?"

Sally shook her head.

"No, we're doing this together. Now come up with a place."

"Well, there's always that place across the street."

"What place?"

"That one," God pointed. A large dome stretched into the sky, behind an impressive white facade. St. Peter's Square stretched out in front, with the familiar statues of saints Peter and Paul flanking the stairs to the entrance.

"Isn't that – the Vatican?"

"Yeah."

"What the hell is it doing in Jamaica?"

"I don't know if the Vatican is really in Jamaica, or if Jamaica is in Vatican City, technically."

"Either way – that's not right."

"Relax," said God. "This kind of thing happens all the time. I'm sure there's a good reason."

"Which would be…?"

God shrugged. "I could look it up."

CHAPTER THIRTEEN: THE ANGLICAN CHURCH DEVELOPS A SERIOUS ATTITUDE PROBLEM

"Damn it!" said the Archbishop of Canterbury, "Those stinking Catholics. Having a cool headquarters like the Vatican just wasn't enough. Now they had to go and move it to Jamaica." His secretary shrugged and the Archbishop sighed.

He turned off the TV and turned to face his secretary, Lilith. If he were head of some other religion, people might look askance at his having a female secretary. Luckily, the Church of England was beyond such concerns. Most of his parishioners' spiritual concerns centered around tea and biscuits, and of course their favorite football club. The gender of the Archbishop's secretary ranked just below where they could find a truly comfortable pair of shoes in their list of religious questions.

At any rate, Lilith was not exactly a sensual creature, even if the Archbishop had been interested. Her impassive demeanor tended to give people the subtle but distinct impression that she was actually an android sent by an alien planet to blend in and monitor human behavior in preparation for a coming invasion. In truth, she simply had a genuine disinterest in the rest of humanity, sexually or otherwise. Her hair, short and tidy, gave the impression of being in a bun, even though it was not. Her impeccable posture and stern expression tended to make people sit a bit straighter and talk more formally in her presence.

The Archbishop, on the other hand, was known for his informality. He liked to joke that the entire Church of England would go down in flames if he didn't have Lilith to keep him organized. Lilith never laughed at this joke. She was too aware of the truth of it.

"How is our Piety Program going?" said the Archbishop. "Any progress there?"

"Unfortunately not, sir," said Lilith. "Our clergy still rank 17th in piety. Catholics and Lutherans are still tied for first. We are five points behind fans of Wisconsin football when it comes to piety."

"We lost a point?"

"Yes," she said. "I'm afraid your latest encyclical caused us to drop."

"Why?"

"It seems people thought the inclusion of a biscuit recipe contributed to an overall lack of theological weight."

"But they are delicious!"

Lilith ignored him. Her lips thinned as she continued with her report.

"People also seem to think our ministers lack moral gravitas."

"Still? I thought our 'This Time, It's Serious' campaign was going to fix that."

"It might be more effective if we could keep our ministers off the society pages. Or the police blotter, for that matter."

The Archbishop looked over the numbers and sighed. He leaned back in his chair and rubbed his temples.

"What will it take to convince people we're a real religion?" he said. "I'm sick of playing second fiddle. Or what was it again - 17th fiddle?"

"Anglicanism is a real religion," said Lilith. "There's no doubt about that. It was created because a king wanted a divorce, but it's still real. At least as real as Scientology."

"Yes, I know you're right," said the Archbishop as he settled back in his chair, his arms behind his head. "But I just wish there was some way we could get on a level playing field with those high and mighty Catholics."

The Archbishop spat out the word 'Catholics' like it burned in his throat. Lilith raised her head and gazed evenly across the table. A slight, hard smile appeared on her face.

"I know sir," said Lilith. "But that may be getting a little harder. We just got news that God is getting married at the Vatican."

The Archbishop sighed and rubbed his eyes. His lips quivered and his hands shook. He pulled himself together and smiled grimly.

"So that's the way it is, huh? God is getting married and not only does he not call, but he is having the wedding at the Vatican."

The Archbishop took a deep breath and sighed heavily.

"Where do we go from here?"

"Well," Lilith said evenly. "Why don't you declare a Holy War on the Catholics? The Catholics have done it enough times. Turn the tables on them, let them feel the pain for a change."

"You know, you may be right," the Archbishop said. "We've been pushed around long enough. We'll make sure God's wedding is one he will never forget."

CHAPTER FOURTEEN: COMING TO AMERICA

In a stunning turn of events, the Anglican Church put forth a press release announcing the beginning of a Holy War with the Catholic Church. In this press release, the Archbishop of Canterbury is quoted as saying, 'Cry Symbolic and let loose the Dogs of Holy War!' His secretary, Lilith, was more composed, adding, 'We must not fear the Catholics. Catholics are the mind-killer. Catholics are the little-death that bring total obliteration. We will face the Catholics. We will permit them to pass over us and through us. And where they have gone past, we will turn the inner eye to see their path. Where the Catholics have gone there will be nothing. Only we will remain. Our Father, the Sleepers have awakened!' In his response to this news, Pope John Paul Georgianringo said, 'What the hell?' though it isn't thought that he was speaking literally. George Stephanopoulos, our holy war correspondent, has more on this story. George, what the hell is this all about and what is the Vatican going to do about it?

The Pope turned off the TV and turned to his advisors, huddled around a conference room table that was slightly too small to fit all of them comfortably. The overall visual effect was less of an imposing war tribunal and more of a poorly planned PTO meeting. The Pope, of course, claimed the head of the table and the TV occupied the foot. Cardinals Tito and Wilson were on the left side of the table, while Cardinals Jermaine, Genesayqua, and 'Bud' were squeezed into the right.

"Now exactly what the hell was that all about and what are we going to do about it?" said the Pope.

"I think George Stephanopoulos was just about to tell us, sir."

"I don't want to rely on a newscast to relay key points to me about an event about which I should already be well-aware. That is why I have advisors. To make me seem more informed than I really am."

The Pope slammed the remote control onto the table and glared at his advisors. The advisors shifted uncomfortably in their seats, looking at each other, trying to see who was going to speak up first.

"Well, sir," said Cardinal Wilson. "it seems the Anglicans have declared war on us."

"I know that. What are we going to do about it?" said the Pope.

Cardinal Jermaine elbowed 'Bud' as Jermaine tried to lean forward to look at the initial report of the Anglican announcement. His chair wouldn't quite allow him enough room and Jermaine pushed himself back and glared at Cardinal 'Bud.'

"Come on now, man," said Jermaine. "What are you doing?"

"Sorry," said 'Bud.' "I'll try to scootch over."

"Why don't you go get us some more wine?" said Cardinal Tito. "Do something useful."

'Bud' nodded and slunk out of the room. Jermaine grinned and reveled briefly in his newfound elbow room. Cardinal Tito stood and took control of the meeting.

"We haven't had a good Holy War for awhile, so I'm afraid we're out of practice." Cardinal Tito said. "I think we need some serious training."

"You mean, Tae-Bo?" said the Pope, giving the air

what he thought of as a solid karate kick, but really it made him look as though he was picked last for kickball as a child.

"No, not Tae-Bo," said Tito. "I for one think we should initiate Plan 9 immediately. I've already contacted Code Name: Diamondhead. He'll be here in 24 hours. He's bringing Rasputin with him."

Tito handed out copies of Plan 9.

"Rasputin?" the Pope said. "Do you really think it's necessary to bring him in? He wasn't always the most reliable monk and he must be a million years old by now."

"Unfortunately sir, it's our only option at this point," said Tito. "Otherwise we'd just fail miserably, like every Eddie Murphy movie since *Coming to America*."

"What about the *Shrek* movies?" said the Pope. "Those were pretty good."

"Yeah, but he didn't have a starring role," said Tito. "Plus, he wasn't even really in it, just his voice. It doesn't count. Besides, that's not really the point. The Anglicans will show us no mercy."

"God help us all," the Pope said.

"I think that's what this whole thing is about, sir."

CHAPTER FIFTEEN: GERMAN SEX

The Archbishop rubbed his hands gleefully. His face was etched with what seemed to be a permanent smile. The announcement of the Anglican Holy War had gone better than he could have hoped. The Archbishop had appeared on all the important serious news shows: Anderson Cooper, Larry King, and *60 Minutes*. Other than the time when Ellen had danced through most of his segment, the interviews had maintained the level of dignity he had intended.

Lilith arrived in his office, armed with paperwork detailing their approach to the Holy War. She handed one copy to the Archbishop and kept the other for herself as she sat down across from him. She straightened the papers in her stack.

"How is everything proceeding with our Holy War?"

"Our spies at the Vatican have reported that the Pope has approved Plan 9, involving agent Diamondhead and possibly one other agent. We aren't sure just yet what this plan involves, or who this other agent is, but I think it's going to be big. I think we need to take special precautions, especially with God's wedding coming up soon."

"You mean - Plan 9?"

"Yes. Strange that our plan has the same identifier as theirs. Maybe we should change ours," Lilith shuffled through stacks of papers, looking for another option. "We could call it Plan 6."

"No," said the Archbishop. "That sounds too much like sex. Especially in German."

"Why German?"

"Because in German, six is sechs, which sounds a lot like sex."

"But why are we speaking German?"

"We aren't."

"So why does it...never mind," said Lilith. "How about Plan 13?"

"Don't be silly, that's bad luck."

"Plan 12?"

"Tempting, but I feel like it should be an odd number."

"OK, Plan 15."

"I'd prefer a prime number."

"But nine isn't a prime number."

"Yes, but it is a prime number squared. Three times three. More prime than prime. Prime squared."

The Archbishop held his hands up, his thumbs and forefingers together forming a square in the air. Lilith shook her head.

"OK, fine," Lilith said. "I really don't think it matters, does it?"

"I guess not. Let's stick with Plan 9."

"Done. At any rate, I think we need to call in Rowdy Roddy and Rasputin. I think they should be able to handle any threats from the Catholic side and they both know Plan 9 inside and out. Plus Rasputin might be able to help us out with counterintelligence from his years in the Catholic's Soviet operations."

"Is Rasputin trustworthy? He is a Catholic, isn't he?"

"Yes, he is. Was." said Lilith. "They kicked him out years ago for having some unusual opinions."

"Fine. Just be sure. We can't be embarrassed by a rogue agent."

"Yes sir." Lilith left the office and made the necessary arrangements. Rowdy Roddy and Rasputin would arrive within the hour. The Catholics wouldn't know what hit them. Lilith smiled, pleased with her foresight. Everything was proceeding as planned.

CHAPTER SIXTEEN: WHO IS THAT TALKING?

The following day, with Plan 9 initiated, the Pope leaned back in his chair, pontificating to his advisers about the advisability of eating vegetables at least twice a day. The Cardinals hunched over the table, dutifully taking notes.

"Corn is good," the Pope declared. "Green beans are bad."

"Sir, I just don't agree," said Wilson. "I like green beans."

"Fool! Have you never heard of Papal infallibility?" said the Pope. "I'm never wrong."

"What about that time you mistook Prince Charles for Charles Manson?" Cardinal Genesayqua said. "You sure were wrong then."

"Yeah, and what about that time you thought Bosnia was in the Middle East?" Wilson said.

"And when you said that the children should go on a crusade?"

"And when you said that you thought Jimmy Carter would be a good President?"

"And when you said-"

"Enough!" said the Pope, slamming the table with his

fist. "You've made your point. But my point was that the yellow tasty goodness of an ear of sweet corn is far superior to the disgusting aftertaste of green beans. And come on, any idiot could think of more creative name than green beans. I mean, how'd they come up with that one? Let's see: they're beans, they're green. No creativity at all. Why didn't they name them something else, like Death Pods from Venus?"

After an awkward pause, Wilson spoke up again.

"Green beans aren't from Venus sir."

The Pope sighed and ran his fingers through his hair. He pulled at his hair just a little bit before releasing it. He took a deep breath before responding.

"I know that. That's my point. They aren't from Venus, so calling them Death Pods from Venus would be creative. Why don't you people listen, instead of just wandering around the Vatican like so many lost sheepherders? I give up."

The Pope threw his hands in the air. He glanced at his agenda for the meeting and decided to move on to the next item.

"Are Rasputin and Diamondhead ready yet?" said the Pope.

"They were due to arrive today sir. We've sent the Popemobile to pick them up."

"That's just great. Send the Popemobile. Why didn't you just take a big sign saying, 'The Pope's secret agents against the Anglicans are here. Feel free to shoot them.'"

"Well, if you really think that'll help, I could arrange it."

"Idiots! Every one of you. Well, I guess it's too late now. Have them meet me in my quarters when they arrive."

CHAPTER SEVENTEEN: WHY EVERYTHING USED TO BE IN LATIN

The Archbishop of Canterbury was deep in thought. "Hmmm," he thought deeply. "What if the only reason we die is that we accept it as an inevitability?"

"Sir!" Lilith said, breaking the Archbishop out of his daze. "Where are you?"

"I'm on the can," he yelled. "Just a minute."

The Archbishop flushed the toilet and emerged from the bathroom. Lilith was waiting in his office. She sat staring across his desk, not moving an inch. The Archbishop paused for a moment to see if she would make any movement. She did not, until the Archbishop coughed and Lilith looked toward him. The Archbishop forced a smile and slid past her to sit down.

"OK now," said the Archbishop. "What do you have for me?"

"I have good news. We think we have positively identified the Catholic agents, though it seemed too easy."

"Really? Why is that?" The Archbishop said.

"Well, they were picked up from the airport in the Popemobile," Lilith said tentatively as she handed him the briefing she had written.

"Hmm," The Archbishop stroked his 'Transubstantiation is BULL' pendant as he looked over the papers, considering this news. "How very clever, yes, how very clever indeed."

"How's that sir?"

"Well you see, it's all very ingenious. Our friends at the Vatican are trying to trick us. I think they think I'm an idiot. You see," said the Archbishop as he stood and began pacing the floor. "They had these two men picked up by the Popemobile, even going so far as to have the chauffeur hold up a sign saying, 'The Pope's secret agents against the Anglicans are here. Feel free to shoot them.' They, believing us to be naïve and foolish, did this to make us think that the secret agents were here. However, we, not being naïve and foolish, would never believe that the secret agents were here, and they, knowing that we are not naïve and foolish, only tried to make us believe that the agents were here to make us believe they were not here, which of course, is not true, because they are here, though I think they think that we think they aren't."

Lilith stared at the Archbishop. "I have no idea what you are saying to me right now."

"Ah, but that's the beauty of it, for neither do I, and if neither I nor you know what I am saying, then how could the Vatican even possibly have the slightest chance of deciphering it?"

"Amazing," said Lilith.

"Thank you, sometimes it's difficult to maintain the level of opacity of language necessary to sustain a religion. Even Archbishops need moral support you know. It's tougher fighting a Holy War against the Catholics than I thought it would be. Ah well. So, how are our own secret agents coming?"

"Well, we're not quite sure," Lilith said. "Agent Rowdy is on schedule to arrive any minute, but we seem to have lost track of Rasputin. It seems he accidentally got in the wrong limo at the airport."

"So where is he then?" said the Archbishop.

"Well," Lilith said as she carefully pretended to read from the briefing in order to avoid eye contact. "The Vatican."

"What?" said the Archbishop. "How in the hell did he get there?"

"As near as we can tell, he got his orders mixed up and thought he was supposed to report directly to his post in counterespionage within the Vatican."

"Irksome," he said to himself. "Well, I guess we'll have to make the best of it. Relay his orders to him. Don't try to extract him. Just get them to him. Tell him to keep low until we need him."

"Yes, sir," Lilith turned to go.

"And Lilith," The Archbishop called after her.

"Yes?"

"Be careful. We don't want the Catholics to find out they have an Anglican in their midst."

"No, sir."

CHAPTER EIGHTEEN: ANY STORY IS IMPROVED BY CLINT EASTWOOD

"Damn it," said Cardinal 'Bud' Nielsen. "Why is it that I'm always the one sent on wine runs when the church runs out? No one ever pays any attention to me any other time."

Cardinal Nielsen had never realized that you really undermine your authority when you put 'Bud' in quotes in the middle of your name like that. So he kept trudging toward the nearest grocery store, with rain soaking him the entire trip. Damned weatherman never got anything right. He was still swearing like a sailor when he found the wine aisle.

'Bud' shook his head sadly. He needed wine for Mass, but the grocery store had only V8. He shrugged. It would have to do. 'Bud' hated V8. He paid for it and turned to leave when he came face-to-face with Clint Eastwood.

"Uh, excuse me," said 'Bud.' "I didn't see you there, Mr. Eastwood."

Clint only stood there squinting at him, not budging an inch.

"My most humble apologies," said 'Bud.' "Please

excuse me."

Clint kept squinting.

"Hey, buddy, what the hell do you think you are doing?" the shopkeeper called out to 'Bud.'

Cardinal 'Bud' Nielsen gestured towards Clint Eastwood.

"I'm trying to leave but Clint Eastwood won't get out of my way."

The shopkeeper fumed, walked over to Clint, and tore him in half.

"It's a cardboard cutout," he said to Cardinal Nielsen. "What are you, some damned moron or something?"

"No," said "Bud." "I'm from the Vatican."

"Huh, it figures," said the shopkeeper. "Sure are a lot of freaks running around the Vatican."

The shopkeeper turned back to his work. 'Bud' decided that it was time to get his eyes checked and went to the nearest optometrist, after having first mistakenly gone to an obstetrician. We won't discuss the details of that experience.

As 'Bud' waited for the doctor to return with his test results, he looked around the office, bored. He also didn't understand why he had to take off his clothes and put on a paper gown that kept coming open in the back to get his eyes checked, but he was no doctor. He hummed along with the Musak playing in the background, an instrumental version of In-A-Gadda-Da-Vida played by an orchestra of violins and oboes. After the organ solo and the drum solo (now violin and oboe solos respectively), the optometrist returned and sat grimly in front of Cardinal Nielsen. He had some bad news.

"Bud," he said. "I have some bad news."

"What is it, Doc?" 'Bud' asked. "Are the Jackson Five back together?"

"No," the doctor said. "I'm afraid you have Chickenvision."

'Bud' shook his head.

"I don't think so, Doc," 'Bud' said. "I don't get cable."

"No, no, that's not what I mean," the doctor said. "You know how you can see all around you without turning your head, but you can only see in two dimensions?"

"Yeah. So?"

"That's not normal. You have the seeing ability of a chicken."

"Does that mean some chicken somewhere has the seeing ability of a Cardinal?"

"Depends on what kind of cardinal you're talking about," said the doctor. "But that's neither here nor there. The point is, you have a serious vision problem."

"Okay," said 'Bud.' "What do I do now?"

"Well," said the doctor. "I'll give you a prescription for some special glasses. But you must realize that due to the unique nature of your problem, these glasses will look extremely silly. You might get made fun of."

'Bud' thought for a second. "I get made fun of now."

"Yes," said the doctor as he scribbled the prescription. "But now you'll get made fun of because of your silly-looking glasses."

'Bud' thought for a moment. "You know, doc, that might be a step up for me."

The doctor shrugged.

"Whatever. I've just got to let you know. Federal regulations. Oh, and as a part of the therapy, you'll have to drink V8."

"I hate V8," said 'Bud.'

"Everybody does," said the doctor as he wrote 'Bud' his prescription.

'Bud' rose and left the office after receiving his extremely silly-looking glasses. The glasses gave onlookers the distinct impression that something wasn't quite right and that the 'something' was probably the guy in the silly glasses. Bud returned to the Vatican with the wine (or really, the V8). The other Cardinals were in the rec room watching football. The Saints were playing the Cardinals and of course the Cardinals were losing.

"Hey, Bud," said Cardinal Jermaine. "Have a Bud."

He handed 'Bud' a beer.

"Uh, thanks," said 'Bud.' "I brought the wine. All they had was V8."

"That's great, man, but we decided to make do with beer," said Cardinal Jermaine.

He paused, swerved to the left, then to the right, then lurched straight at Cardinal 'Bud' Nielsen.

"You know," said Cardinal Jermaine. "You've got some serious beer goggles."

He snatched Bud's glasses from his face and put them on.

"Whooo-hoo!" said Jermaine. "Where's the women?"

The rest of the Cardinals pelted Jermaine with pretzels and beer nuts.

"That's right," said Jermaine. "I forgot. This is the Vatican. There aren't any wo-"

Cardinal Jermaine passed out. 'Bud' stepped over him, put the wine away, and went up to his chambers. Behind him, the other Cardinals howled as the Saints ran it in for another touchdown.

CHAPTER NINETEEN: A BIG HAT MAKES YOU SEEM TALLER

Rasputin and Diamondhead stood at attention before the Pope in his office. The Pope looked them up and down in admiration. They both stood straight and proud. Rasputin had his long, gray hair tied back, tight to his skull. He couldn't be sure without looking, but he was fairly certain that Diamondhead was sleeping while standing perfectly straight, eyes open and looking straight ahead.

The Pope saluted and told them to stand at ease. Rasputin relaxed. Diamondhead's reaction was a bit delayed, contributing to Rasputin's belief regarding Diamondhead's standing siesta. The Pope handed each of them a plain brown manila folder.

"These are your orders," the Pope told them. "See that they are carried out properly."

The Pope sat down and dismissed them with a wave of his hand.

"And make sure there are no green beans involved!"

Rasputin and Diamondhead looked at the folders and then at each other, wondering exactly what they had gotten themselves into. They both shrugged and exited the room.

Rasputin undid his hair, letting it fall about his shoulders. He glared at Diamondhead.

"Green beans?" said Rasputin as the pair walked down the hall. "What was that all about?"

Diamondhead shrugged. "I don't know. That guy was the Pope?"

"Da."

"Hmm. Somehow I expected him to be taller."

The two fell silent as a third man approached them, dressed in a suit of armor.

"Either of you two seen a Sampo laying around anywhere?"

Rasputin and Diamondhead both shook their heads.

"Damn," the knight said. "I'm running out of places to look. Thanks anyway."

The man hurried down the hall. Rasputin and Diamondhead looked at each other and shrugged again.

"Sure are a lot of freaks running around the Vatican," said Diamondhead.

"Da," said Rasputin, sighing.

The pair left the Vatican and looked for a place to eat lunch. They bought some jerk chicken with breadfruit from a stand and found a nearby bench so they could sit and eat. It was a beautiful day, the oppressive heat and humidity had taken the day off; replaced by a gentle warmth almost completely empty of breeze. Rasputin and Diamondhead reviewed their orders.

"You know," said Rasputin, as he munched on his chicken thoughtfully. "This plan is terrible. I've seen a lot of bad plans, back in the Soviet days, but this is worse than any of them."

"Oh, I don't know," said Diamondhead. "I think it's pretty good. It made me laugh, it made me cry. I give it four stars out of five."

Rasputin stared at Diamondhead for a moment, considered his options, and decided to ignore him.

"Khristos, look at it," said Rasputin. "I'll probably get

killed four or five times over. I don't think my body can take that kind of punishment. Maybe in my forties, but now? Nyet."

"Peas and carrots, peas and carrots," sang Diamondhead as he ate his breadfruit.

Rasputin shook his head in amazement. He didn't understand how he was supposed to work with someone like Diamondhead.

"What I mean is," Rasputin continued. "how is it that we're supposed to defeat the Anglicans with two empty manila envelopes?"

Rasputin looked at Diamondhead, who seemed to be considering it.

"I wonder if I could make my envelope into a Pope hat," Diamondhead said. "Then I'll be the one to give the orders."

Rasputin only shook his head. He was glad that he wouldn't have to put up with Diamondhead the whole time. All Rasputin needed to do is wait Diamondhead out. Rasputin knew that when the time for Plan 9 came, Diamondhead would be irrelevant. After years of waiting, it would finally be his time, Rasputin's time. He would not allow someone like Diamondhead to stand in his way. Rasputin would crush Diamondhead, if it came to that, like Ivan Drago in the first part of *Rocky IV*.

CHAPTER TWENTY: YOU REALLY CAN GET A POPE BOBBLEHEAD

The Archbishop was just beginning to brief Agent Rowdy for his mission. He perched on a stool, leaning atop an overhead projector, the kind that is no longer used in sufficiently funded school systems.

"This is your contact in the Vatican," the Archbishop said as he brought up an image of Rasputin on the overhead. "You will use the sign 'Hi, how's it going?' and he will respond with the countersign 'Fine. And you?' Got that?"

Rowdy nodded, bent over his notebook, dutifully taking down everything that the Archbishop said.

"Good. Make sure you write all this down. I don't want you forgetting anything," said the Archbishop. He changed slides. "This is your first objective: To neutralize the Pope and his advisors. The Pope is the one on the left in the funny hat, then Cardinals Tito, Jermaine, Geneseyqua, 'Bud,' and Wilson. With them out of the way, we should have no trouble stopping God's wedding."

Rowdy looked up, squinting at the picture. He scrunched up his nose and turned to the Archbishop with his hand raised.

"The one on the left is the Pope?" said Rowdy.

"Yes."

"Hmmm. I thought he'd be taller."

"Well, keep in mind, they will all be significantly bigger than in these pictures. Almost as tall as me."

"Almost as tall as me," Rowdy said as he took down the Archbishop's every word.

"You will meet Rasputin inside the Vatican and he will fill you in on the specifics of the rest of Plan 9. Now you should go see Mr. X to be outfitted."

"Mr. X." Rowdy wrote as he got up to leave.

Rowdy went down the hall, where Mr. X awaited him.

"Hello, Rowdy," Mr. X said.

"Hello Mr. X," Rowdy said. "I'm here to be outfitted."

"Ah, yes. Walk this way."

Mr. X walked with an unusual gait, which Rowdy did not imitate, since that kind of joke is pretty played out these days. Mr. X. led him through the room, past many devices being tested, many of which were extremely cool-looking. They stopped at a large oak table that held several items Rowdy couldn't identify. One of them looked really cool.

"These are your supplies," said Mr. X. He picked up something that looked like a common ballpoint pen.

"As you can see," Mr. X said. "This looks like a common ballpoint pen. It functions just as a pen would, except it has one important feature. If you click the pen five times and point it at a wall, then it projects an image of God against that wall. This should cause any Catholics in the area to kneel down, bowing their heads to pray, which will allow you time to escape."

Mr. X handed Rowdy the pen, which Rowdy put into his pocket as Mr. X. picked up the next item from the table.

"This item," said Mr. X. "appears to be a common He-Man Thermos. You can store any liquid, hot or cold, in it, and it will know whether to keep it hot or cold."

"What's special about it?" Rowdy asked, examining the Thermos.

"Isn't that enough?" said Mr. X. "How does it know the difference?"

Rowdy shrugged and put the Thermos down. Mr. X went on to the next item, which appeared to be a common household cleanser.

"This, which appears to be a common household cleanser, is actually a high potency knockout gas. It can be released just by opening the bottle and it should knock out anyone in the vicinity. You can avoid the effects yourself by inhaling the inside of the cap, which makes you immune to the gas. As a side benefit, if you need something to be clean, it has been approved by four out of five dentists. It also gives a nice, fresh, pine fragrance. But don't smell it."

Rowdy handled the bottle, looking at it approvingly. He set it down quickly, however, when he noticed that Mr. X was moving on to the next item, the one that looked really, really cool.

"As you can see," said Mr. X. "This item looks really, really, really cool."

He handed the item to Rowdy, who nodded, impressed.

"What's it do?" Rowdy asked.

"Nothing," said Mr. X. "It's just cool. So cool, in fact, that you could use it in an emergency to temporarily distract your opponents with its coolness."

Rowdy nodded.

"I know what you mean," he said. "That happens to me all the time. People get distracted by my coolness."

Rowdy tossed his head back, and struck an exaggerated pose of nonchalance, the type of nonchalance that tells everyone that the person in that pose really wants you to know how little he cares.

"Yeah, sure," said Mr. X. "Whatever you say."

"I don't care what you say," said Rowdy. "I don't need to know how cool I am to know how cool I am."

Mr. X sighed, then reached into his pocket and pulled out one more item. It appeared to be a button that said, "Transubstantiation is NOT bull," and he pinned it onto Rowdy's jacket.

"This is a button that says, 'Transubstantiation is NOT bull,'" said Mr. X. "Now your disguise is complete."

Rowdy walked over to a mirror and shook his head in awe. No one in the Vatican would recognize him when he carried a pen, a He-Man Thermos, and some common household cleanser while wearing the "Transubstantiation is NOT bull" button, not to mention the thing that looked really, really, really, really cool. The Catholics didn't stand a chance.

Agent Rowdy flew from London to Jamaica, busily preparing himself for his mission. He began by familiarizing himself with the equipment Mr. X had given him. As it turned out, he needed the practice. He knocked himself out with the common household cleanser at least six times before he remembered where the antidote was and he nearly blinded himself when he peered into the end of the pen while turning on the laser projection of God.

Setting the items aside, Rowdy opened the large manila envelope that contained the specifics of his assignment. He frowned as he leafed through the sheets of paper. The papers only had one word per page, comprising a single sentence in total. Put together they read, "Go to the Vatican to chew bubble gum and kick ass." Either that or, "Chew the ass to go Vatican and to kick bubble gum," but Rowdy rightly assumed such orders didn't make any sense. He was to go to the Vatican to chew bubble gum and kick ass. There was a problem, Rowdy realized. Mr. X had never given him any bubble gum.

'Oh well,' he thought. 'At least I can still kick ass.'

Agent Rowdy drove up to the Vatican and knocked on the door. He waited for awhile and finally Cardinal Tito answered the door.

"My name is Rowdy," said Agent Rowdy. "and you ain't seen nothing yet. I'm here to see the Pope."

"Oh, okay," Tito said and gestured for Rowdy to enter.

Rowdy followed Cardinal Tito through the Vatican halls until he found himself standing in the Pope's office. The Pope gestured for him to sit down. The Pope turned back to his computer and began typing. A Pope bobblehead figurine danced wildly on top of the Pope's monitor. After a few minutes, the Pope shut off his computer and turned to face Rowdy.

"So, Rudy," he said.

"Rowdy."

"That's what I said. What brings you here?" the Pope asked as he leaned over his desk.

"Well," Rowdy said slowly. "I've always wanted to be a Pope and so I thought I should study under the best."

The Pope smiled and leaned back in his chair. He reached behind his head to open the mini-fridge and took out two cans.

"What do you think qualifies you to be Pope?"

"Let's see," said Rowdy. "I've got speed. I walk so fast, talk so fast, I can turn the light off and be in bed before the room is dark."

The Pope popped the top on both cans and poured each into frosted glasses that also emerged from the mini-fridge.

"Very nice," the Pope said, handing him a glass. "Here, have a V8."

Rowdy hated V8.

CHAPTER TWENTY-ONE: WHERE'S PAT SAJAK WHEN YOU REALLY NEED HIM?

Chuck was pleased. He had just been appointed god, without even a background check or face-to-face interview. It was two in the morning, but he was too excited to sleep. Chuck was typing at his computer and planning his first acts as god. Sarah McLachlan blared from his speakers. Sure, something heavier like Zeppelin or Black Sabbath might have been more appropriate, but McLachlan was as heavy as Chuck had.

'First, I will take revenge on everyone who ever called me a dork in high school,' he thought. 'Then I'll have to remember to alphabetize my comic book collection within categories and make sure to double bag my *Punisher #4*.'

Chuck sat back from his computer and smiled. He wondered why anyone would quit such a fantastic job. Sure, he had only been god for a couple of hours, but the potential job satisfaction seemed limitless. Being god promised all the power Chuck had sought in his former life as a mad scientist, without all the mucking about with electricity and chemicals and whatnot. It was all *Caddyshack* and no *Caddyshack II.*

'That reminds me,' he thought. 'I'll have to see what kind of pension plan I get for this.'

The subtle whoosh of a letter floating through his mail slot interrupted Chuck's planning. He picked up the letter. It was addressed simply to 'Chuck' with no address and no return address. He frowned, then opened the letter. It read, in friendly, cheerful print:

Dear Chuck,

Congratulations on becoming the new god. We are looking forward to working with you in the coming years. Please be sure to submit all reports, expenses, and paid-time-off requests in a timely manner.

Have a nice day!

Chuck flipped the letter onto his desk and decided to check on his people to see how everything was going. Looking over the list of disciples the previous god had left him, Chuck decided to start at the top. Unfortunately, Pat Sajak was not available. Cursing silently, Chuck went to the next name on the list. He went to the airport and took the first flight out to the Vatican.

When Chuck arrived at the Vatican, he brushed past the guards and proceeded directly to the Pope's office. The Pope was sitting behind his desk and a man that Chuck didn't recognize sat in a chair in front. The Pope looked up at Chuck and narrowed his eyes.

"Can I help you?" said the Pope.

"I'm the new god," said Chuck. "I'm here to check in, see how things are going."

The Pope nodded distractedly as he reach for another can from the mini-fridge. He poured another glass and handed it to Chuck.

"Here," the Pope said. "Have a V8."

Chuck hated V8.

"Pardon me if I seem distracted," said the Pope as he stirred his V8. "But I'm currently fighting a Holy War with the Anglicans. It's taken all my focus."

The Pope picked up his smartphone and cackled madly.

"Look at that cat!" he said. "He is not happy about being in that Santa hat."

The Pope continued to laugh as the man next to Chuck stood up. The Pope and Chuck looked at him quizzically.

"I came here to chew bubble gum and kick ass," said the man. "And I'm all out of bubble gum."

He then took a He-Man Thermos out of his jacket, opened it, and threw the contents on the floor. Beef vegetable soup spilled everywhere. The Pope and Chuck stared at him blankly.

"Damn it," Rowdy said, throwing the Thermos to the floor in disgust. "Wrong bottle."

He then took out with a flourish what appeared to be a bottle of common household cleanser. He unscrewed it, threw the cap to the ground, and breathed deeply from the bottle. He was out cold in seconds.

"What the hell was that about?" said Chuck.

The Pope shrugged. "I think the green beans may have gotten to him somehow. Tragic really. He said he wanted to be the first Pope named Rowdy."

"Yes. Very unfortunate," said Chuck, not sure what he was talking about.

"I'll see that he gets the care he needs. I'll have Tito show you to your room now," the Pope said to Chuck.

Cardinal Tito poked his head inside the door and gestured for Chuck to follow him down the hall.

"That was the Pope?" Chuck asked.

Tito nodded.

"Somehow I expected him to be taller."

Tito only shrugged. They approached a door at the end of the hallway and Tito gestured to it.

"In there?" Chuck asked.

Tito nodded.

Chuck entered cautiously, then relaxed when he saw the room. It wasn't much, but it would do. Chuck examined the television, seeing it had cable.

"Cool!" he said. "This place gets the *Playboy* channel."

Chuck had just sat down to watch *The Edible Panty Murders* when there was a knock at the door. He rose to answer it and was rather embarrassed when he realized two things. First, Vanna White was at the door. Second, he wasn't wearing any pants. Though, he thought to himself, how many opportunities does a man get to be in a room with Vanna White without his pants on? Very few, he thought, and so he regarded himself as very lucky.

"Hello," said Chuck. "Have you been helped?"

"No, I haven't," Vanna said. "Is Pat here?"

"Pat?" said Chuck. "Pat who?"

"Pat Sajak, of course," said Vanna. "Is he here?"

"No," said Chuck. "Should he be?"

Vanna looked for a number on the door in vain.

"Is this 1313 Mockingbird Lane, Los Angeles California?" she asked.

"No," said Chuck. "This is 1313 Mockingbird Lane, Vatican City."

"Oh," Vanna said, embarrassed. "Sorry to trouble you."

And Vanna left.

Chuck considered his situation. He was now alone without any pants on. Somehow the situation had degenerated rather quickly. Chuck decided that, as god, he didn't have to put up with this type of thing and decided to go out for a bite to eat. He decided to go to the nice little Italian bistro he had seen across the street. Unbeknownst to him, he walked through a bizarre dent in the fabric of space-time which had inadvertently placed said Italian bistro across the street from the Vatican despite the fact that the bistro was quite clearly located in Jamaica.

Chuck entered the restaurant and sat down at the bar. Sitting next to him was a rather impressively built Viking. Chuck was fully prepared not to notice this odd fact, but was prevented from doing so. The Viking in question did not like not being noticed and so made himself known to Chuck by lifting him up by the collar.

"Don't worry," said the bartender. "He's just being friendly. That's his way of saying hello."

Chuck turned his head in the Viking's direction and weakly extended his hand.

"Hello," he croaked. "Very nice to meet you."

The Viking shook his hand vigorously and set Chuck back down on the stool.

"Buy my friend here a drink!" Thor said to the bartender. The bartender poured liquids from various bottles into a glass and handed it to Chuck.

"Why, thank you," Chuck said. He picked up the glass and downed it in one gulp. "Mmm. That was very refreshing."

Thor stared at Chuck incredulously. "Bartender! Another round."

The bartender fixed two more drinks. Chuck again downed his immediately. The Viking attempted to match him, but stopped when his hand began to twitch. He finished with his second gulp. This continued for awhile. I'd tell you about each one, but trust me, it would get tedious very quickly. Kind of like a Carrot Top HBO special.

"Barterndner!" Thor said. "Annnuther dreenk for my frie…" He passed out.

"Well," said Chuck. "I guess he's had enough."

Chuck ordered himself a steak and his dinner continued uneventfully. He rose when he was done and went back to the Vatican. On his way out of Giovanni's, he saw his former assistant, Frank, drooling on someone's foot. Chuck kicked Frank in the stomach and went on his way.

CHAPTER TWENTY-TWO: AND THAT'S WHERE WE GET EGGS BENEDICT

Cardinal 'Bud' Nielsen emerged from his chambers. It was time to report to work. Cardinal 'Bud' was on babysitting duty, as the other cardinals called it. 'Bud' puttered down the hall to the Pope's office. 'Bud' entered to find the Pope standing over an unconscious man, clapping his hands over him in an attempt to wake him up. The unconscious man began to stir. 'Bud' walked over and stood over him as he woke up.

"What happened?" 'Bud' asked. "He drink too much?"

"No, no," said the Pope, waving his hands. "Green beans."

"Right," Cardinal 'Bud' said. "But what's that got to do with-"

"Wow," the formerly unconscious man said, sitting up and blinking himself awake. "I have got to stop doing that."

"Sure do," said the Pope, nodding. "Very few people who are unconscious make it to the level of Pope. Except Pope Benedict, but that was a very special case. Political."

Cardinal 'Bud' and the Pope helped Rowdy to his feet.

"Rowdy," the Pope said. "I'd like you to meet, eh, Willis."

"'Bud,'" said 'Bud.' "My name's not Willis."

"See the hat?" snapped Rowdy. "That means he's the Pope and you're Willis."

"What you talkin' about, Rowdy?" said 'Bud.'

"He's the Pope."

"So what?"

"So buttons." Rowdy clutched his "Transubstantiation is NOT bull" pendant as he glared at 'Bud.' "I'm starting to think you're one of them."

"One of who?" said 'Bud.' "The Drummonds?"

"No," said Rowdy. "The Anglicans."

"Come on now, boys," said the Pope as he walked over to the bar. "Let's just calm down and have a drink. Here." The Pope handed each of them a glass. "Have a V8."

Rowdy and 'Bud' hated V8.

CHAPTER TWENTY-THREE: TRUST ME, RAGNAROK IS NO PICNIC

Frank awoke, face down on the floor of the bar. Some drool had congealed on the side of his mouth and his cheek was stuck to the floor. He kept his eyes closed, fearing the light. Frank sat up, shaking his head to clear his mind. He opened his eyes slowly, adjusting to the light. Thor looked down at him from the bar stool and extended a hand.

"Please," Frank said, on his knees, hands in the air. "No more. I just want to go home."

Thor laughed. "It's OK little man. I think you've had enough. You've been sleeping there for a few days, you know."

"What?" said Frank. "Days?"

Thor nodded.

"Yes, I'm afraid so," said Thor. "I haven't seen someone pass out so hard since the time Loki convinced me to cross-dress to fool Prymr into marrying me. It wasn't my proudest moment, but Prymr was sure surprised when he saw me wielding Mjollnir. He passed right out."

Frank nodded and Thor helped him to stand up. Frank

sat at the bar next to Thor, grabbed a glass of water, and dumped it over his own head.

"I had to do that too," said Thor. "Some mortal came and drank me under the table. It took a few more than one though. I woke up a little faster too."

"Really?" said Frank. "You?"

"Yeah, I couldn't believe it. Some little scientist guy named Chuck. Incredible."

"Chuck?" Frank choked. "Chuck was here?"

"Why? You know him?"

"Unfortunately," said Frank. "He used to be my boss. He fired me. He said I wasn't evil enough."

"In his defense, you don't look that evil."

"I'm not, really," Frank ran his fingers through his hair. "So I can't blame him. And really, that is what brought me here today, sort of. You see, I'm looking for God. He visited me looking for Pat Sajak and ever since then I've been on a mission to find him."

"Well, you've come to the right place. Plenty of gods right here. Why, I'm a retired god myself. I was a Scandinavian god of thunder for a long time. Watch this."

Thor got up, raised a glorious golden hammer, swung it into the floor, causing a massive thunderbolt to careen through the bar. The other customers ducked, then clapped appreciatively. Thor gave a small bow, then turned back to Frank, who had covered his head with his arms. Frank carefully peered out.

"Very nice," said Frank. "Are you done now?

"Yes," said Thor, putting his hammer back in his coat. "I decided to retire before the giant snake killed me at ragnarok."

"Sure, sure, I can see that," said Frank, who wasn't sure what was going on. "You never want to be killed at Reagan's Rock."

"Ragnarok."

"Either one, really."

Frank stood up and made a valiant, but fruitless effort

at straightening his clothes. His hair dripped with water and Frank looked every bit as hungover as he felt. And he felt very hungover.

"Well, Thor, it's been real, but I've got to get going. I'm looking for the big 'G' God, not any old god that comes down the pike. Or is it pipe?" Frank shrugged. "Either way, my mission isn't over. Want to come with?"

"Eh, what the hell," said Thor. "There's more to life than drinking. After all, there is always fighting."

CHAPTER TWENTY-FOUR: GOOGLE HERBERT GROENEMEYER

"Great Scott!" said Diamondhead.

"What is it?" asked Rasputin, looking around fervently. "Anglicans?"

"No, no," said Diamondhead. "I was just practicing."

Rasputin glowered. He wished that God's wedding would hurry up and arrive already. Diamondhead was already getting on his nerves. The hotel they were staying at was nice, but living in close quarters with Diamondhead took away a bit of the beauty of the sea just outside their room. The small patio was just enough for the two of them to sit comfortably with a table between them, just large enough to hold a pot of coffee. Rasputin took a drink of coffee and concentrated on the crashing of the waves for a moment. The coffee didn't help much, since it was just the free coffee that came with the room. It was better than nothing, but not by much.

"Well, quit it," said Rasputin. "We've got work to do."

"Right, right," said Diamondhead as he glanced sideways at Rasputin. "What was that again? Something about wiping out the Anaheim Angels? I mean, seriously, are we working for George Steinbrenner or what?"

An intense, burning desire crept through Rasputin's body to reach out, tear out Diamondhead's tongue, and wear it in his lapel. He resisted the urge and concentrated on keeping his voice level.

"No," said Rasputin slowly as he counted to ten in his head. "We work for the Pope. We're fighting the Anglicans."

"Right, right," said Diamondhead. "Now, Rasputin, why are we still in Vatican City? Shouldn't we be out infiltrating the Anglicans, or Anglicizing the infidels, or something by now? It's no wonder I forgot the plan. What is the plan again?"

Rasputin sighed and poured himself another cup of stale coffee.

"Plan 9," said Rasputin. "You made it into a Pope hat."

"Oh yeah," said Diamondhead. "That was fun. What now, Rasputin? I'm up for anything: Chutes & Ladders, Checkers, No Limit Hold 'Em?"

"I told you before," said Rasputin, sighing heavily. "Not to use my real name. We're supposed to always stick with our cover story. I'm Wolfgang Amadeus Groenemeyer and you're Lou Ferrigno's cousin Javier."

"Right," said Diamondhead. "I'm Javier Ferrigno and you're Wolfgang Puck's cousin Amadeus."

"No, no," said Rasputin. "That isn't quite right. I'm nobody's cousin, I'm just Wolfgang Amadeus Groenemeyer. You are Lou Ferrigno's cousin, Javier."

"Oh, OK, I get it now. I'm Javier, cousin of Lou Ferrigno. But you don't have any cousins."

"Why don't we role play a little bit, make sure you have it down?"

"OK," said Diamondhead. "You be Carl Reiner and I'll be Mel Brooks."

"No," said Rasputin, shaking his head. "You're Javier and I'm Wolfgang. That's what we're role playing. Pretend we just met someone. Introduce us."

"All right," said Diamondhead. "We can do the 6,000-year-old-man routine later. Ahem. Ahem. 'Good evening, madam. I'm Javier Ferrigno and this is Wolfgang Amadeus Groenemeyer. He has no cousins.'"

"Good," said Rasputin. "Except you don't need to say that I don't have any cousins. You're the one with the cousins."

"But you just said you didn't have any cousins. I was just being precise."

"Yes, but you don't need to say that. It's weird. And you didn't even mention that you were Lou Ferrigno's cousin."

"Of course not," said Diamondhead. "I don't want to be a name-dropper. I wouldn't just go around trading on my cousin's good name like that. If it came up in conversation I wouldn't deny we were related, but I'm not just going to offer up the Hulk unprompted. How rude, to say something like that for no reason."

"But you said I didn't have any cousins and there was no reason for that!"

"Yes," said Diamondhead patiently. "But no one's ever tried to get seated in a restaurant by telling the maitre'd that he didn't have any cousins. It's not the same."

"Fine," said Rasputin, grimacing as he clenched his fists. "It doesn't matter. Let's just get to work. We really should have things planned out by now."

"Wolfgang," said Diamondhead. "There's something I've been meaning to ask you."

"Yes?"

"What the hell is an Anglican anyway?"

Rasputin sighed and started walking toward the water. Diamondhead started to follow, but Rasputin put a hand up, stopping him.

"I'll be back," said Rasputin. "You stay here."

CHAPTER TWENTY-FIVE: THE HOLY CORN FLAKES OF ANTIOCH

Cardinal Jermaine entered the Pope's office as 'Bud,' Rowdy, and the Pope finished their toast of V8. 'Bud' and Rowdy looked slightly ill. The Pope, however, was smiling broadly.

"Cardinal Jermaine," said the Pope. "I'd like you to meet Rowdy – he wants to be the next Pope. The dapper gentleman to his left is Willis."

"Actually, it's 'Bud,'" said 'Bud.'

"Don't start with that again," said Rowdy. "Who here is the Pope?"

Cardinal 'Bud' rolled his eyes.

"Come on now," said Rowdy, poking his index finger in Bud's chest. "Who here is the Pope? Are you the Pope?"

"No."

"Who's the Pope?" Rowdy glared at 'Bud.'

'Bud' shuffled his feet uncomfortably. "He is."

"Right. And is the Pope fallible?"

"What do you mean?"

"What do you mean, what do I mean?" said Rowdy.

"What?"

"Oh never mind," said Rowdy. "You're Willis, end of story."

"Jermaine," said the Pope. "Could you show Rowdy to a room? He is joining us as a new Cardinal."

Rowdy followed Jermaine through the hall to his room. Rowdy sat back in an orange easy chair and considered his progress. On the upside, he was well on his way to becoming the first Pope named Rowdy. On the downside, he was supposed to chew bubble gum and kick ass, not become the first Pope named Rowdy. Plus, he'd spilled his beef vegetable soup.

In any case, he was pretty hungry. Rowdy listed his options to himself. He could A) Quit the Anglicans and become the next Pope, B) Sneak out of his room, grab a snack, and proceed with the ass-kicking, as planned, or C) Try to find a date, or, failing that, a mint condition *Punisher #4* he could keep in a plastic bag.

Rowdy carefully considered the pros and cons of the various options until fate intervened: Rowdy's stomach grumbled noisily. He went to the door and cracked it open. He gathered his household cleanser, He-Man Thermos, and ballpoint pen and peered into the hallway. The coast was clear.

Rowdy crept down the hall, carefully checking each door, trying to find the pantry, which hopefully would contain Hi-C and Nutter Butters, or, at the very least, some of that marshmallow stuff that comes in a big jar and stays in the back of your cupboard for seventy-five years. As he continued his search, he remembered that he had forgotten the really really cool thing.

'That's weird,' thought Rowdy. 'I remembered I forgot something. How does that work? Later will I forget that I remembered I forgot it?'

Rowdy considered going back for it, but decided against it. His He-Man Thermos, ballpoint pen, household cleanser and 'Transubstantiation is NOT bull' button would have to be enough to successfully complete his mission, find a sandwich, or both.

Finally, Rowdy came to the pantry door. He opened it quietly. He debated whether or not to turn the light on, but decided against it. Instead, he clicked on the ballpoint pen and searched for sustenance by the warm glow of God projected onto the Corn Flakes. Surprised by someone coming in, Rowdy ducked into a closet and hid.

Cardinal Mollari, the eldest of all the Cardinals, entered the pantry slowly, with the assistance of two canes he carried with him. As the pantry door swung shut behind him, he realized he was face to face with God's image, still being projected onto the box of Corn Flakes. Cardinal Mollari cried out and ran down the hallway as best he could, calling for help. Rowdy slunk out from behind the closet door, grabbed the pen, turned it off, and quickly made his way back to his room, silently cursing his luck. All that creeping around and still no Nutter Butters or marshmallow fluff.

Cardinal Mollari gathered everyone he could find and rushed back to the pantry entrance.

"It's in here," he said. "Here, I present to you, the Holy Corn Flakes, graced with God's image!"

He swung the door open with a flourish and pointed inside with one of his canes. The other Cardinals gathered around the door and peered in, only to find Cardinal Wilson sitting at the table, polishing off the last of the Corn Flakes.

"Oh my God!" said Cardinal Mollari. "What have you done?"

Cardinal Wilson looked up from his bowl, his mouth full of Corn Flakes, and milk dripping down his chin.

"What?" he said. "What's the big deal?"

CHAPTER TWENTY-SIX: REBECCA LOBO COULD KICK YOUR ASS

Cardinal 'Bud' Nielsen was glad to make it to the end of his shift babysitting the Pope. He was still getting over his embarrassment at having his extraordinarily silly-looking glasses stolen by the other Cardinals and needed some time to himself. It wasn't so much the actual taking of the glasses, but the way they made fun of him as he jumped around like a girl trying to get them back as the others played keep-away. Not like a talented, future WNBA girl either, but like a girl who would avoid volleyball in the future for fear of great embarrassment.

'Bud' left the Vatican and made his way to Johnny's bar for a drink. It was still early, but 'Bud' couldn't wait. He moped in the door and peered into the bar. It was pretty empty. The jukebox echoed off the walls and glasses clinked behind the bar as the bartender cleaned. 'Bud' paused in the doorway then took a seat at the bar, two seats down from the only other customer in the place.

'Bud' nodded towards the man as he took his seat. The man wore horn-rimmed glasses, corduroy pants, and a green cardigan sweater over a light yellow shirt. He smiled and nodded back at 'Bud' and took a drink. 'Bud' ordered a Chardonnay and picked up a book of matches from the bar. He struck a match and let it burn for a second before throwing it into the ashtray. His wine arrived and 'Bud' struck another match and flicked it again into the ashtray.

"Keep that up and you'll burn the whole place down," chuckled the other man.

'Bud' glanced at him and smiled ruefully. He put the matches down and took a drink of wine. He winced slightly. The wine was just a bit too dry for his taste. He put the wine down and turned his attention again to the other man.

"Sorry," said 'Bud.' "Just releasing some stress."

"What's got you stressed?"

'Bud' shrugged. He hung his head and rubbed his forehead with his fingertips.

"I don't know," he said. "It's my job, I guess. None of my coworkers are very supportive."

The man nodded and slid down a seat to the stool next to him. He extended his hand.

"I know the feeling," said the man. "My name's Buddy."

'Bud' smiled in surprise and suppressed a chuckle.

"It's nice to meet you, Buddy," he said. "I'm 'Bud.'"

Buddy laughed and the two shook hands. In a silent moment 'Bud' took another sip of wine as Buddy looked into his eyes.

"It's hard for guys like us, isn't it?"

'Bud' tilted his head to the side and narrowed his eyes. A weak smile emerged on his face.

"What do you mean?"

Buddy peered over his horn-rimmed glasses and raised an eyebrow.

"OK," said the man. "Let's put it all out there, shall we? You're gay, aren't you?"

'Bud' grimaced and shook his head.

"No," said 'Bud.' "I don't think so."

Buddy leaned back and smiled.

"Well, have you ever considered it?"

'Bud' rubbed his temples.

"Well, no," said 'Bud.' "Not really."

Buddy leaned in slightly and briefly touched 'Bud's' knee.

"Then how do you know? Have you ever kissed a girl?"

"No," said 'Bud.' "But I once got aroused by an episode of Golden Girls."

"Which one?" asked Buddy.

"The one where Bea Arthur bosses around a plumber. I've never wanted to be a plumber so much in my life."

Buddy smiled, clasped his hands, and rested his chin on his index fingers. He took a drink of his beer and exhaled as he set the glass back on the bar. The jukebox clicked behind them and a new song blared through the speakers.

"I love this song," said Buddy.

"Yeah, Weezer is awesome," said 'Bud.' "You know, you kind of look like Buddy Holly."

Buddy smiled and leaned in.

"Does that make you Mary Tyler Moore?"

'Bud' leaned back and spread out his hands.

"What am I supposed to do?" asked 'Bud.'

Buddy smiled and took 'Bud's hands in his.

"Come on, Mary," said Buddy. "I don't care what they say about us anyway. Let's play that funky music."

"I think you're confusing Buddy Holly with the lead singer of Wild Cherry."

"No, Mary, I'm not. Come on, kiss me."

Buddy leaned in further and kissed 'Bud' on the lips.

"Say," said 'Bud.' "If I squint just a little, you sort of look like Bea Arthur."

CHAPTER TWENTY-SEVEN: WHO'S JOHNNY? SHE SAID

Frank and Thor walked slowly down the side of the road, thumbs out, as car after car passed by. The sun beat down on them and the whistle of cars rushing by threw up dust and dirt.

"This sucks," said Frank. "Why won't anyone stop?"

Thor shrugged and kept walking. Frank let his arm fall to his side. His backpack slung over one shoulder, he peered down the road.

"Where the hell are we going anyway?"

Thor shrugged again. "How do I know? This is your mission, not mine. This God of yours: Where does he usually hang out?"

Frank threw his hands up in the air.

"I don't know. I don't even go to church."

"Church?" said Thor. "Where's that?"

"You know," said Frank. "A building where people go to worship."

Thor shrugged again. "Sorry," he said. "Never been the religious type."

"But you're a god," said Frank.

"Yeah," said Thor, scratching his beard thoughtfully. "But not like today. We were old school. Running around, drinking and fighting. Generally causing trouble. Not like the reserved, straight-laced gods you find more often today."

Frank mulled that over. "Didn't your worshippers have anywhere to go to pay homage to you?"

"You kidding?" said Thor. "My worshippers wouldn't know what 'homage' means."

Thor kneeled and picked up a clod of dirt. He crushed it in his fingers, letting the dirt fall between them, back to the ground. He glanced back up at Frank.

"What does 'homage' mean anyway?"

"Don't worry about it," said Frank. "It's not important."

Thor shifted from foot to foot. "Still," he said. "It seems like we should be doing something."

"Yeah," said Frank as he bit his lower lip. He closed his eyes.

"What are you doing?" said Thor.

"I'm trying to think of where I would go, if I were God."

Thor paused for a moment.

"Is it working?" said Thor.

"Not really."

"Well," said Thor. "We could always go to Johnny's."

"Johnny's?"

"Yeah, down the street," said Thor. "Some of the gods hang out there. Not really my thing, mainly a piano bar. Kind of cheesy."

"You think God might be there?"

Thor shrugged. "Could be. Does your God like music?"

"Well, hymns and stuff yeah. Is it religious music that Johnny sings?"

"Sort of," said Thor. "Let's go check it out."

Johnny's was the premiere nightclub in all of Vatican

City. Every priest, nun, or novitiate who was anyone would go there to see and be seen. The ceiling featured a recreation of the Sistine Chapel ceiling, except in Johnny's version, Eve is significantly curvier and instead of an apple, she is offering Adam a bottle of wine and a smile. Johnny wailed into the microphone as Frank and Thor entered, "I think I love Jews, so what am I so afraid of? I'm afraid that I'm not sure of, a religion with no Jesus…"

Frank and Thor took a seat at the bar. Frank cocked his head, listening to the lyrics, as Johnny continued to sing.

"What is this music?" said Frank.

"That's Johnny's thing," said Thor. "He rewrites pop songs to make them into religious songs."

"So that's his version of The Partridge Family?"

"I guess. I'm not a huge fan."

"Of Johnny," said Frank. "Or of The Partridge Family?"

"Either one."

Frank shrugged and turned to get the bartender's attention. The bartender pretended not to notice him as long as he could and Frank started to get angry. He pounded the bar with his fists.

"Barkeep!" he bellowed. The bartender reluctantly walked on over.

"What is it?" he said.

"Why were you ignoring me?" Frank asked.

"Well, buddy, you look like hell. What do you expect?"

Frank surveyed his appearance in a mirror hung behind the bar. He did look a bit frazzled, with dirt from the road covering his clothes and his hair a bit of a mess. He tousled his hair, trying to get it to look respectable again.

"Even so," said Frank. "We're paying customers and we want something to drink."

"Fine," said the bartender. "So what do you want?"

Frank squinted behind the bar.

"I'm not really sure," he said. "Thor, why don't you go ahead?"

Thor turned away from the stage, where he had been watching Johnny perform his update of an '80s classic, "She Blinded Me With Scientology."

"What?" said Thor. "I wasn't paying attention. I didn't know we were ordering drinks."

"Well of course we are," said Frank. "Why else would we be in a bar?"

"I thought you were looking for God."

Frank's face froze, then his jaw slackened. On stage, Johnny was just finishing up the last verse of "Buddha Man," his take on "Barbara Ann." Frank pulled himself together as Johnny started into his remake of a Neil Diamond hit, "Coming to Valhalla."

"Yes, of course you're right," said Frank. He turned to the barman. "Nothing to drink then, but we're looking for someone and I wonder if you've seen them."

"I see a lot of folks," said the bartender. "Can you be more specific?"

"Of course," said Frank. "We're looking for God."

"God?" said the bartender. "God who?"

Frank was temporarily distracted at the sight of Thor dancing up a storm. He whirled around the dance floor, his hair flowing from underneath his horned hat, and Mjollnir threatening to fly off from its spot on this belt. Apparently, "Coming To Valhalla" was a favorite.

The bartender snapped his fingers and waved to get Frank's attention. "Come on, buddy, I don't have all day. God who?"

Frank was stumped. "What do you mean, God who? God, that's who."

The bartender turned up his hands. "Doesn't ring a bell. What's she look like?"

"What does he look like," Frank corrected. "God's a man."

"Yeah OK," said the barman. "Whatever gets your Bible thumping. So what's he look like?"

Frank thought for a moment, his index finger on his

chin, eyebrows furrowed. "That's a tough one," he said.

"Tough one?" said the barman. "How is that a tough one?"

"You see," said Frank. "I've never met him personally. So any description may be inaccurate."

"Don't you have any description?" said the barman. "How would you know him if you found him?"

"That is a problem," said Frank. "I do have a very general description. Long white hair, beard. Tallish, I imagine."

"Is that him?" the bartender pointed to a man seated near the front of the stage.

Frank peered through the poorly lit bar, squinting to see, even though squinting doesn't really help, since it's practically closing your eyes, so how could that help you see, but everyone does it just the same. He managed to make out the man the bartender was pointing out. He did have white hair and looked to be on the tallish side, but no beard, at best some scruff.

"No, no," said Frank. "I don't think so. More Charlton Heston, less Jimmy Buffet."

Frank had no way of knowing that the man actually was Jimmy Buffet. Jimmy stopped in at Johnny's whenever he played a concert at the Vatican. After the show, he and Johnny would usually troll for open-minded women. They usually came up short, since they mostly ran into nuns, who tend to be something less than open-minded on the topics of most interest to Jimmy and Johnny. Those nights would usually end up with Jimmy and Johnny back at the bar, drinking and singing Ave Maria to the tune of Margaritaville until the neighbors complained. Then they would switch to singing Margaritaville to the tune of Ave Maria until the cops came. After the cops came, they would usually field requests from the crowd since, let's face it: Cops have guns.

"If that's not him, he isn't here," said the bartender. "You might want to stick around and ask Johnny. He seems to know everyone worth knowing. He should be due for a break soon. He's been singing all night."

Thor had left the dance floor, since Johnny had moved on to a showy stage set for his Styx cover, "Come Pray Away."

"So what's the word?" said Thor. "Any luck yet?"

'Yet' is the twenty-four-thousand seven hundred ninety-first word in the story so far, counting hyphenated words as two, of course, and including chapter titles. In celebration of this landmark, we will continue the story at the point at which Thor and Frank meet Johnny. The only things that happened in between are that Thor dances some more, both of them order drinks, and one of them accidentally spills his drink.

I'd tell you how the drink came to be spilled, but it really is a boring story of no consequence whatsoever. I hesitated even to mention it in the first place, but if I hadn't, one might wonder why Frank's pants had a stain on them later and get all confused. Don't get overly concerned with the stain, as it is also of no consequence whatsoever. We continue.

Thor and Frank followed Johnny into his office. Johnny's office was nice, not as gaudy as you might expect from a performer. Very tasteful, in fact. Not nearly as Elton John-y as you might have guessed from Johnny's stage persona. Johnny gestured for them to sit down, then frowned.

"What happened to your pants?" he asked, gesturing to the stain on Frank's pants.

"Oh that," said Frank, brushing his pants with his hand, even though the stain was from a liquid and brushing a liquid with your hand really does nothing except rub the stain in even more. Or at least that's what my mom says. "It's not important."

Johnny shrugged. "OK then. What did you want to discuss?"

"God," Frank said. "Or to be specific, if you knew

where God was."

Johnny leaned back in his chair and put his feet on his desk. He pointed to a picture hanging on the wall just behind his head.

"See that?" said Johnny. "That's me with Buddha and Frank Sinatra."

He reached over to grab a glass from his desk. He eyed it suspiciously, then took a cautious sip. Satisfied that the drink passed inspection, he downed the rest of it.

"I tell ya," Johnny said. "Don't get those two together unless you don't have any plans for the next couple of weeks."

"Now that you mention it," said Thor. "I don't really have anything..."

"Very nice," said Frank before Thor could finish. "But we're looking for God."

"That's the point," said Johnny as he put his feet down and leaned across the desk.. "The point exactly. That...." Johnny said, turning to pour himself another drink.

"....is exactly the point, I couldn't have said it better myself."

Johnny leaned over to the stereo and punched up his duet with Frank Sinatra, "That's Why the Lady is a Virgin." He snapped his fingers to the music, closing his eyes for a moment.

"Excuse me," said Frank. "But I don't think that is the point. I mean, it is the point, but you don't seem to be addressing the point in question."

"What question?"

"Where is God?" said Frank through clenched teeth. "That question."

"Oh," said Johnny. "That question." He sat up, his eyes fixed on the speakers.

"Wait, wait, Frankie baby," Johnny said. "Here comes the good part."

Johnny stood and began waving his arms as if he were conducting the music. He was really into it, eyes closed, arms gesticulating wildly but expertly to the music. As the music faded, he sat back down and turned back to Frank and Thor. Frank had to give it to Johnny: that had, in fact, been the good part.

"So what's the answer?" said Frank. He elbowed Thor in the ribs. "You want to help me out here?"

"What?" said Thor, as he broke out of his daze. "Oh yeah."

Thor looked around, then tightened his grip on his hammer and leaned in over the desk until his eyes were only inches away from Johnny's.

"Where is God?" Thor said.

"That's the point, baby," said Johnny. "He's right here."

Frank looked around, confused.

"Where?"

"Everywhere, baby, everywhere," Johnny gestured back to the photo on the wall. "Frank Sinatra is god to some people. Some people think Buddha is god, though strangely enough, Buddhists don't. The point is, god is everywhere and everyone. Someone somewhere might even think of you as a god."

Johnny looked Frank up and down. "A god of squalor, I imagine."

Thor leaned back in his chair and ran his hand through his hair, his horned hat on his lap.

"Look, mister," said Thor. "I'm a god myself. I've had millions of followers. But Frank's not looking for just any old god, but one specific God. So can you help or what?"

Johnny spread his hands out in front of him.

"What do you want from me?" said Johnny. "You guys come in here, looking for some god, you've got no description, no nothing. No idea of what you're doing. Can't you tell me anything about this guy? It's kind of weird to be so desperate to find someone you can't even describe. What's your story?"

Frank thought for a moment. He took a deep breath

and closed his eyes briefly.

"I can tell you all I know. I'm not sure if it'll help," he said. He took another deep breath. "It's a long story, but I think Pat Sajak sent God to crap on my couch. One day God appeared at my front door, asking for Pat Sajak. He came inside, crapped on my couch, then left when he realized he had the wrong address. I tracked him to his home in a trailer park in Jersey, but he had already moved to Jamaica, so I followed him here. Jamaica ends up being right next to the Vatican for reasons I don't fully understand, though I do realize it makes things a heck of a lot easier on everyone involved. We came here since it seems like all the gods either hang out here or at Giovanni's."

"If he was in your house," said Johnny. "Why don't you know what he looks like?"

"He was in the form of a dog at the time," said Frank. "A Cavalier King Charles Spaniel, I think."

"You don't have any kind of description then?"

"Well," said Frank. "He has sort of old mannish quality to his voice, somewhat curmudgeonly, not nearly as much like James Mason as you might expect. He doesn't have a name really, except some people call him Yahweh sometimes, and he's Jesus's dad."

Johnny slapped his desk.

"Oh," said Johnny. "That God! Why didn't you say so?"

Johnny pointed to another picture of himself, God, Jesus, and another fellow playing a concert together. Jesus was setting his guitar on fire, while God was about to stage-dive, wearing a red headband, no shirt, and tight black leather pants. Johnny was on drums, while the other guy played bass. It looked like a pretty rocking show, judging by the number of pairs of panties that had been thrown on the stage.

"That's me playing with God and his band, Trinity. Say what you want about the Holy Ghost, but he can really play the bass. God is not Jesus's dad though. That was just a misunderstanding. When Trinity first started to get popular, the group was interviewed by one of the local papers. The reporter asked them how it felt to be stars. Jesus said he wasn't a star: He was the sun. From then on, everyone called Jesus 'The Sun.' At some point, the spelling got messed up."

Thor and Frank left Johnny's a few minutes later with a flier for Trinity's next gig, Friday night. They also scored backstage passes after being a bit overly generous with the tip jar on Johnny's desk. Finally the stage was set for Frank to meet God face to face.

CHAPTER TWENTY-EIGHT: WHERE DO WE GO FROM HERE?

Rowdy frowned at the Reuben sandwich he had gotten from Giovanni's takeout window. It wasn't what he thought a Reuben should be. He had expected it to be toasted, with Thousand Island dressing and Rye bread, but it came grilled on pumpernickel bread with Russian dressing. He might have been better off trying to get back into the Vatican pantry, but he decided one fiasco per day was enough.

As Rowdy finished the sandwich, he considered how he should proceed with his quest to infiltrate the Catholics. He needed help. That was clear from his botched attempt at finding Nutter Butters. Then he remembered the sign/countersign he had been given to make contact at the Vatican. With his repeated bouts of unconsciousness and his excitement at potentially becoming the next Pope, he had forgotten about meeting his contact. Unfortunately he couldn't remember his contact's name or what he looked like. But he did remember the all-important countersign.

Rowdy hurried back to the Vatican, anxious to meet his contact and figure out their next steps. As he entered, he slowed, looking around for someone to whom he could give the sign and hopefully get the countersign. He found Cardinal Tito sitting in the Cardinal's lounge reading a book. Rowdy approached him in what he hoped was a stealthy, but not too stealthy manner.

"Hi, how's it going?" said Rowdy, giving the secret sign he had been given at Anglican headquarters.

"Fine," said Cardinal Tito as he closed his book and looked up. "And you?"

Rowdy smiled inwardly. It was the right countersign. He had found his contact. It had been a lot easier than he had thought it would be.

"Great," said Rowdy. "No complaints."

Rowdy looked around in what he hoped was a furtive, but not too furtive manner. He sat down next to Tito. He glanced around again, then leaned in towards him.

"So," said Rowdy. "What do we do now?"

"What do you mean?" asked Cardinal Tito.

"Is there someplace private we should go?"

"Are you coming on to me?"

"What?" said Rowdy. "Of course not."

"Then why should we go someplace private?" asked Cardinal Tito.

"You know," said Rowdy. "That thing."

Rowdy nodded and gestured wildly, in a way in which he hoped said 'We're part of a secret plot to spoil God's wedding, thereby taking the Catholic Church down a notch,' but that really said 'I'm a complete lunatic, get away as fast as you can.'

"What thing?" said Cardinal Tito.

Rowdy decided to take another route. He grabbed what appeared to be a common He-Man Thermos, a common ballpoint pen, a bottle of common household cleanser, and his button that said "Transubstantiation is NOT bull." He held them up, framing his face in a circle of stuff.

"Here," he said. "Don't these things suggest anything to you? What type of person might carry these things around?" Rowdy smiled broadly and nodded, raising his eyebrows suggestively.

Cardinal Tito regarded the items one by one, along with Rowdy's somewhat manic expression and concluded the obvious: Rowdy was completely insane.

"I guess it does suggest something…" said Tito, somewhat at a loss.

"OK, then, I thought it might," said Rowdy. He leaned toward Tito and whispered. "So where do we go from here?"

CHAPTER TWENTY-NINE: REST IN PEACE, MICK SHRIMPTON

Sally and God approached the Vatican, intending to check it out for the wedding ceremony. As they approached the steps, God stopped short.

"Shoot! Is today Thursday?"

"Yes." Sally replied.

"Damn it! I'm late for rehearsal. Again. Man, Jesus is gonna be pissed."

"Rehearsal? What for?"

"My band. Trinity. We have a gig tomorrow night. We really need to practice because I've totally been spacing on it this week."

Sally stopped and shifted her weight, looking between God and the Vatican.

"I completely forgot that you were in a band. You have a gig tomorrow night? Why didn't you mention this before we made plans?"

"Dude, I had a good reason," said God. "I told you: I spaced."

"What kind of band is it?"

"We're still finding our identity, but we really take our

110

inspiration from Spinal Tap."

"Spinal Tap? So what, your amps all go to eleven?"

"Hey, don't do that," said God, shaking his head. "Don't make a joke of them. Spinal Tap are geniuses. Especially Peter Bond and Mick Shrimpton before they spontaneously combusted in 1982."

"Even so, I would have thought your band would be Christian rock."

"Yeah, right," said God. "No way. Even Jesus hates Christian rock. It doesn't improve Christianity, it only makes rock worse."

Sally nodded and shifted her weight as she looked up the stairs toward the Vatican.

"So where is this concert of yours?" she said.

"At the National Arena, here in Kingston."

"Really? That place is huge!"

"Yeah, well," said God. "Not in the big arena, technically. We'll be in the indoor arena part."

Sally furrowed her eyebrows.

"You mean the practice field?"

"That's not its official name," said God. "It's called the Indoor Arena. We would be playing the big arena, but it was already booked."

"By who?"

"Color Me Badd."

Sally laughed.

"Whatever," said Sally. "But do you have to go now? We're supposed to meet the Vatican people right now."

"It won't take long," said God. "We'll bang out a few songs and be back here in a couple of hours. I'll call the people at the Vatican from the cab and let them know we'll be there in a bit. Just let me borrow your phone."

"OK, I guess," said Sally. "But you owe me big."

"I know," said God. "Don't worry, I'll make it up to you. We'll get Rod Stewart to sing at our wedding."

"Why Rod Stewart?" said Sally. "That's how you are going to make it up to me?"

"I thought all women loved Rod Stewart," said God. "Loved to see him shake his booty, so they can throw their underwear at him."

"He's like, 70 years old," said Sally. "He might appeal to my mom, maybe, but I doubt even women her age want to see Rod Stewart shake it anymore. Besides, even if I did like Rod Stewart, I wouldn't throw my underwear at my own wedding reception."

"OK, OK," said God. "Not Rod Stewart. Train, Night Ranger, whoever you want then. Can we just go?"

"Train, are you kidding? Why not just get Coldplay?"

"Do you like Coldplay?"

"No. No one likes Coldplay."

"OK. So we won't get Coldplay. And no Rod Stewart. But Night Ranger is still on the table?"

"We'll talk about it later."

God and Sally jogged to the street and hailed a cab.

As they got out at the Holy Ghost's house, God grimaced. The driveway was empty.

"That's not good," he said. "Jesus's Camaro isn't here."

God and Sally went into the garage, where the Holy Ghost sat tuning his guitar and playing the bass line of "Good Feeling" by the Violent Femmes. It was pretty impressive. The bass line to "Good Feeling" is difficult enough, but to play it while tuning a guitar is a real feat. I doubt even Brian Ritchie could do that.

"Hey dude," said God. "Where the hell is Jesus?"

The Holy Ghost shrugged and switched to the bass line from "Sweet Emotion."

"Gone, man," he said. "Said he'd had it with you. Said he was going to try to get the Apostles back together. Unless Judy is still holding a grudge."

The Holy Ghost turned to look at Sally, narrowing his eyes.

"And who is this?" he said. "Yoko?"

"Come on, man," said God. "Leave her alone. It isn't her fault. I'm the one that spaced. What about the show tomorrow?"

The Holy Ghost shrugged again.

"I don't know, man," he said. "I suppose we could put Johnny on drums, if you could handle lead guitar. Of course, you won't be able to stage dive like you normally do. But at least we won't have to cancel."

"That's cool," said God. "Looks like it'll be our final show anyway."

"Looks like it."

God picked up a guitar and plucked each string individually, making sure each was in tune.

"But I guess we still need to practice. Call Johnny while I limber up."

CHAPTER THIRTY: MARSHMALLOW FLUFF

After he walked down the beach to clear his head, Rasputin refocused on what he needed to do next. Given that Plan 9 was composed of several blank sheets of paper, Rasputin thought that gave him license to freelance. Instead of going to Church House to infiltrate the Anglicans and figure out their plans, Rasputin guided Diamondhead back to the Vatican. Best of all, Diamondhead was too dim to notice. They hid in the Vatican pantry while Rasputin considered what to do next. Luckily, Diamondhead had found some Nutter Butters, giving Rasputin some time to weigh his options.

As he watched Diamondhead scarf down his food, Rasputin had a possibly brilliant, but potentially dangerous insight. His biggest problem could be his biggest asset: Diamondhead. Rasputin decided to take the risk and use the somewhat unorthodox approach of lying to Diamondhead's face.

"So, Diamondhead," said Rasputin. "Now that we're here at Church House, what do you think we should do next?"

Diamondhead stopped eating, forgetting to swallow for a second. He choked, gagged, then washed down the Nutter Butters with some milk and looked across the table. Not surprisingly, he was dumbfounded. It was hard to tell the difference, but Rasputin's keen eye was able to discern the minute difference between Diamondhead looking dumbfounded and Diamondhead looking dumb.

"This is Church House?" said Diamondhead, looking around. "I thought this was the Vatican's pantry."

"It does look that way," Rasputin nodded. "The Anglicans just copied the Vatican's design. Couldn't even come up with their own HQ."

Diamondhead looked around in awe. "That's amazing! This is exactly like the Vatican's pantry, down to the last detail. They even have that jar of marshmallow fluff that sits on the top shelf year after year. Those stupid Anglicans. They deserve whatever it is we're here to do to them, or for them, or whatever."

Diamondhead slammed his fist on the table, bouncing the plates and Nutter Butters an inch in the air. For a moment, Rasputin thought he looked as focused and dedicated as a young Muhammed Ali refusing to go to Vietnam. He was almost moved, until Diamondhead's head tilted to the side and he raised a finger in the air.

"What is it again that we're doing here exactly?"

Rasputin sighed. Now was the time to get Diamondhead headed in the right direction. It would take all of Rasputin's patience and focus to keep Diamondhead on the path and not distracted by Nutter Butters, paper Pope hats, or an opportunity to play the part of Mel Brooks in the 6,000 year-old man routine. Rasputin was still concentrating deeply when a knight poked his head into the pantry.

"Hey guys," said the knight. "Have you seen a Sampo around anywhere?"

Rasputin and Diamondhead shook their heads.

"Damn," said the knight. "Thanks guys."

He left.

"Sure are a lot of freaks running around Church House," said Diamondhead.

Rasputin thought that was the smartest thing he'd ever heard Diamondhead say. A crease appeared in Rasputin's forehead. Rasputin had begun to rely on Diamondhead's unfathomable stupidity. Soon, it would all happen. Plan 9 was taking form and would soon be fully deployed. This was no time for Diamondhead to start thinking. Diamondhead picked up a Nutter Butter, sniffed it deeply, and started choking on the crumbs that had flown up his nostrils as he inhaled. Rasputin smiled inwardly. Plan 9 would work. Diamondhead would not get in the way. Rasputin could hardly wait.

CHAPTER THIRTY-ONE: GODS DO NOT WAIT

The line buzzed with excitement as Thor and Frank waited outside the National Indoor Arena for the Trinity concert. Some of the buzz had been due to a rumor that Color Me Badd had unexpectedly released another block of seats for their show, but that rumor had proved unfounded. Rumor also had it that Jesus wasn't going to show up, but Trinity would put on a great show regardless.

There was a lot more at stake for Frank than mere musical appreciation. For Frank, it would be the culmination of an arduous journey: He will have found God himself. I almost said 'epic' journey instead of arduous, but those jerks that label every mildly funny cartoon they see on the internet as 'epic' ruined that word for me. It's too bad, because describing Frank's journey as epic would have been consistent with its actual meaning, unlike using it to refer to a mildly funny cartoon.

Thor, on the other hand, was not nearly as excited about the concert. He peered over the line to get in, shifting his feet impatiently. He sighed.

"Gods don't wait in line," he muttered.

Frank glanced at Thor, then glanced at the line.

"I know, but relax," said Frank. "It won't take long."

Thor tossed his hammer from hand to hand, pacing back and forth.

"I hate to wait."

As the line got shorter, Thor got more agitated. Just as Thor seemed to reach his agitation limit and threatened progression to outright frustration, they were at the front of the line. Thor settled into a medium agitation when the ticket taker reached out toward them.

"Tickets, please."

Frank handed the man their tickets, while Thor continued to fume. The ticket taker fumbled with the tickets, struggling with the scanner. He dropped their tickets on the ground and stooped to pick them up.

"Good god, man," said Thor. "What is your problem? Your only job is to take tickets, how hard can that be?"

"Sir, please calm down," said the ticket taker. "I'm getting you through as quickly as I can."

"That," muttered Thor. "Is what I'm afraid of."

The ticket taker tried scanning the tickets, but the scanner wasn't working. Thor paced as the ticket taker called another ticket taker over to use his scanner. Thor boiled at a steady extreme frustration, until finally, their tickets were verified and Thor and Frank were waved through.

"About time," said Thor. "Gods do not wait."

The ticket taker smiled weakly as Thor and Frank passed into the arena.

"Take it easy," said Frank. "We're so close. Don't get us thrown out before we even get in."

Frank and Thor went into the concert hall, finding no seats, but simply a large open area, festival-style. Frank grimaced and Thor glared at Frank.

"Just great," said Thor. "I told you we should've brought a blanket."

"Relax," said Frank. "Everyone stands the whole time

anyway."

"I hate standing," said Thor. "I don't even like their music. They are just another Spinal Tap rip-off band. If you're going to rip someone off, at least make it somebody talented."

Finally, the lights dimmed and the crowd grew quiet. The opening act, The Rosary Beads, came out and started to play. A ska band and not a good one, if there even is such a thing. Thor visibly shook and closed his eyes, holding back the rage that threatened to break out.

"I don't know how much of this I can take."

Ska is often used as evidence of the incorrectness of evolution by creationists. Since ska is a worse form of music than those that preceded it, it logically follows that evolution is not happening, or if it is, it is working backwards. It rarely occurs to creationists that the existence of ska might also be used as evidence against the existence of a benevolent god. If they do think of it, they keep it to themselves.

Luckily, the ska band played only a short set and exited the stage. The crowd grew quiet. Really, they were already quiet, since no one was quite into the ska band, except one guy that kept jumping up and down in front of Thor, threatening to launch Thor's extreme frustration into full-blown anger. I didn't really want to belabor the point, since I've already been pretty hard on ska.

The spotlights shone on the stage. The kick drum started, followed by the bass line. Finally God stepped into the spotlight and started playing. He was on guitar, eager to prove he had the chops to replace Jesus on lead. The stage lit up and the music kicked into high gear. The crowd went wild, clearly the pre-concert grumbling Frank had heard about Jesus being scratched was no longer a concern.

Frank and Thor were the only ones not into the music. Frank was fascinated, but not by the music. Seeing God up on stage had him entranced. Sure, the red leather pants and headband took a little something off the experience and the lesbian couple making out in front of him was a little distracting, but this was still a momentous moment for Frank. He didn't hold it against them though, since "Come To My Confessional" is a supremely romantic song and a Melissa Etheridge tune to boot. Trinity had incorporated some songs from Johnny's repertoire for the evening.

Thor, on the other hand, seemed to get increasingly agitated as the concert went on. He found the ballads especially excruciating, but at no point did he approach enjoying himself. The only way he kept his sanity was through truly vast amounts of beer. By the third song, Thor was already a little tipsy. By the end of the guitar solo in "Crazy Little Thing Called Faith," Thor was three sheets to the wind, which, my grandmother assures me, means he was very, very drunk. She also thinks that if you get your shirt wet while washing dishes at the sink, then you are at high risk for alcoholism. So watch out for that.

Unfortunately, Frank was too enraptured to notice the ill-fated combination of Thor's drunkenness and agitation. By the time the main show ended and the crowd was cheering for an encore, Thor was past his limit, in terms of both alcohol and anger. He stood up and was just about to demand that they leave, when the jumping guy from the opening act accidentally bumped into him. Thor raged and threw the man off him.

The man went flying and crashed through the lesbians, into some guys that had been watching the lesbians make out, drinking, and getting their hopes unrealistically high. They looked up as they rose and locked eyes with Thor. He looked happier than he had all night. Frank tried to get Thor out of there.

"Well" Frank said. "Let's get going. We've got to get backsta-."

He was interrupted by the lesbians scrambling for cover. Where Thor should have been, was a mass of people, some trying desperately to get free, others trying desperately to join the scrum. Fists, feet, elbows, and knees were thrown everywhere and everywhere people were getting new facial features they'd have trouble explaining at work the next day without raising suspicion of some sort of domestic situation. Frank sighed, looked toward the hall going backstage, then back at the scrum. He hesitated, then had his decision made for him, as two guys bowled him over and he fell into the pit of people. He waved his arms helplessly, then curled up to protect himself until it all was over. He could hear God pleading for calm, to no avail. Frank wept.

CHAPTER THIRTY-TWO: WHAT A WANKER

God, Johnny, and the Holy Ghost were ushered offstage, out of the stadium, and into a waiting limo. The limo lurched toward the street, deftly avoiding the masses that were hightailing it out of the stadium. As the limo made it's way to the Holy Ghost's house, God and Johnny were trying to figure out what had happened.

"Dude, what was that?" said God. "I've never seen anything like that before."

"I know, baby," Johnny said. "Crazy. What, did they think they were at a Judas Priest concert or what? I've never seen people riot to Melissa Etheridge songs."

"Seriously. But you should know better than mention Judas to me."

"I didn't say Judas, I said Judas Priest. Christ, what's your problem?"

"Oh great, now you're talking about Christ! He abandoned us tonight, in case you didn't realize."

Johnny shrugged. The Holy Ghost gazed out the window. They pulled up at the Holy Ghost's house and went inside. God and the Ghost cracked open a couple of beers and Johnny poured himself a scotch. He drank it in a gulp and poured himself another. He sighed, took another sip, and looked up at God.

"So what now?"

God shrugged.

"I don't know," said God. "Hopefully, most of our fans will stay out of prison and we'll go from there I guess."

"Or they'll go to one of those women's prisons," said Johnny. "Like on Cinemax."

God looked at Johnny and grimaced. "If I've told you once, I've told you a thousand times. Real women's prisons are nothing like that."

"How would you know?" said Johnny. "You've never been to a woman's prison."

"Are you kidding?" said God. "Are we really talking about this? Now?"

"Hey, you brought it up."

"I did not bring it up, you did, with your little Cinemax fixation."

"No, that was after you mentioned them going to prison."

God fumed and stormed into the living room, throwing himself into a chair. The Holy Ghost lay sprawled across the sofa, his eyes open, following the conversation, but saying nothing. The silence was broken by what sounded like a team of mad baboons pounding at the door. Or how I imagine it would sound if a team of mad baboons were pounding at the door, if you're one of those jerks that points out similes with which the speaker is unlikely to have direct experience, as if people were completely unable to reliably predict something without actually witnessing it. Because in reality, a team of mad baboons pounding at the door sounds nothing like you would expect, but rather sounds like Sting singing one of those stupid bullshit songs of his. Not one of The Police songs, but one of the solo songs, where he's always wearing a turtleneck sweater in the video. What man walks around in a turtleneck sweater? Singing? Come on now. Mad baboons sound nothing like Sting in a turtleneck.

Johnny walked over and answered the door, only to find Sally standing there disheveled, her hair going in all directions, sweating, and her clothes looking ruffled and somehow moist.

"You," she said, pointing at God as she pushed Johnny aside as she strode into the house.

God looked toward the Holy Ghost and Johnny. Both averted their eyes, suddenly very interested in everything except God and Sally.

"I was in the front row, you know. You could've, you know, done something to like, help or something."

"Ever notice you get a little valley-girlish when you're mad?"

The Holy Ghost shook his head at God and waved his hands, but it was too late.

"Don't even start with me," Sally said. "You left me in a crowd of maniacs, people throwing things, running around, pushing, shoving, punching, kicking, screaming. It was a nightmare. And then, then, then! Then I finally fight my way backstage and you're nowhere to be found! Off, in a limo somewhere." She sighed, then gestured weakly to the house around her. "Here, apparently."

She picked up Johnny's glass and smelled it, then pointed to the beer bottles in the trash.

"With your buddies, having a little drink. Not a care in the world. Nice. Real nice. Especially when we're supposed to get married! Like, soon! Unbelievable."

Sally went into the kitchen, opened the fridge, frowned, then closed it again. She returned to the living room, pacing back and forth. God considered his options, while Johnny looked uncomfortable and the Holy Ghost looked confused.

God decided that under the circumstances, his options were few. If he wanted to save his relationship with Sally, he was going to have to do something drastic. He was going to have to grovel like no man had ever groveled before. He would have to grovel really well, not really poorly.

Not like someone who had never groveled before, since someone who had never groveled before probably wouldn't be very good at it. More like someone expert in groveling, that did it as their job, and had been promoted to senior vice-president of groveling. Not someone that was just in it for the money either, but someone supremely motivated by the pure joy of doing some top-notch, world-class groveling. The Mozart of groveling, except without dying so young.

"Sweetie, I'm sorry," said God, quickly crossing the room to put his arm around Sally, only to have her shrug it off.

"Don't sweetie me."

"Let me make it up to you," said God. "Anything you want, you got it. Honeymoon anywhere you want. Whatever. I'm an idiot, a moron, I don't deserve you. A wanker, if you like British insults, which typically sound a little first-graderish to my ears, but hey, I'm not British. Wanker, really, come on now. Wanker. It's fun to say though, but I can't imagine using it when I'm really mad at someone. It's like a pretend-mad word. I think that might be why the British Empire fell, no one took them seriously enough because they kept using words like wanker and bugger when they were mad. But that's not really the point. Just tell me what I can do to make it up to you and I'll make it happen. I'll humiliate myself, worship the ground you walk on, anything you want, and I will make it happen. Just say the word."

Sally shook her head and stomped her foot.

"You don't get it, do you?" she said. "This isn't something you can charm your way out of by being cute. You're not as cute as you think in any case."

God gulped. Johnny stepped in and put his hand on

Sally's shoulder.

"Whatever you do, Johnny," said Sally evenly. "Don't touch me and don't start in with 'baby.' I know you do it to everyone, not just women - but now's not the time."

Johnny removed his hand and forced a smile.

"Sorry, Sally," said Johnny. "I know it's inexcusable, but it wasn't all God's fault. It was crazy in there. The security team was forcing us into the car. With all the commotion, the noise, I'm not sure anyone realized what was going on, who was there, and who wasn't. God asked about you, but no one heard him."

Sally swayed a little and glanced upward at God uncertainly.

"Is that true?"

God looked at Johnny, then back at Sally. He smiled and put his hands up, facing Sally.

"Not entirely," God admitted. "It's true that everything happened super-fast with a ton of commotion. The security guards ushered us into the limo without stopping to think of anything else. But I won't lie. I didn't ask about you. It all happened so quickly. I just didn't think."

Sally let a few silent moments pass. Johnny took the opportunity to disappear, not wanting to face Sally's wrath. For her part, Sally did not seem wrathful. Her anger had dissipated and was replaced by a melancholy disappointment.

God took Sally's hand and looked her in the eyes. Her disappointment was somehow worse than her anger.

"I am so sorry," God said.

Sally wiped a tear from her eye.

"It's just that," she said. "I thought I meant more to you than that."

God took Sally in his arms and stroked her hair.

"You do. You mean more than anything. I just wasn't thinking. You know that's not my strong suit."

Sally laughed through her tears despite herself.

"Aren't you going to make some kind of 1980s pop

culture reference?" she said.

"I can if it would help. Let's see. I feel as bad as Jo did the time she had to admit to Mrs. Garrett that she had shoplifted Mrs. Garrett's birthday present. How's that?"

"Not bad," she said. "I was thinking you'd go *Greatest American Hero* on me. *Facts of Life* was a nice change."

"Well, you know, I've got to keep things interesting," said God. "Just when you think I'm going to zig, I zag."

Sally laughed again.

"You certainly keep it interesting."

God smiled and looked her in the eyes.

"I love you," he said. "And I'll do anything for you."

"Anything?"

"Anything."

Sally smiled and slipped her hand into his.

"Great," she said. "I know just the place."

"For the honeymoon? You name it. Where to? Paris? Mozambique?" God smiled.

"Fred Astaire."

"Fred Astaire? That's person, not a place. A dead person, I'm fairly certain."

"It's a dance studio. We're going to learn the waltz for our first dance at the wedding reception."

God's smile disappeared. He glanced over at the Holy Ghost, who shrugged, then at Johnny, who by this time was fast asleep in the chair. God smiled again, albeit less convincingly.

"Great," he said. "Just let me know when and where."

"Will do," Sally said. She led him toward the door. "Say goodbye to your buddies, we're going home."

"Bye, guys," God said as he walked out the door. "See you later."

The Holy Ghost waved weakly, while Johnny remained unconscious in the chair. God and Sally got into the limo and the car pulled away.

"I really am glad you're OK," said God.

Sally leaned in and kissed him. I'll leave the scene here.

You're probably not too distressed by the things God does in this story if you've read this far, but God getting lucky in the back of a limousine might be just a bit more than you could take. I might have already crossed the line by even mentioning it. If so, sorry about that.

CHAPTER THIRTY-THREE: THANK YOU IN ADVANCE

Chuck fumed in his room. The Vatican rooms were pretty nice and a plaque on the wall said that the Queen of England had once stayed there. The room was tasteful, not as ostentatious as you might expect based on the Pope's headgear. He sat in the oversized chair, drumming his fingers on the arm. The Pope had blown him off and Chuck hadn't become god to be sent to his room while the Pope ran the show.

Chuck was distracted from his anger by a whoosh as a sheet of paper slid underneath his door and settled on the floor. He rose from his chair and stalked over to pick it up. Printed in friendly, cheerful letters, it read:

Hello Chuck!

Welcome to the Vatican! This is just a friendly reminder that reports are due each day by midnight. To date, you are delinquent in submitting your reports. As a courtesy, the deadline for your reports has been extended to the end of the week as you acclimate to the significant responsibilities of your new role. Please be sure to submit your reports prior to this extended deadline to avoid any possible penalties that may result.

Thank you in advance for your full cooperation.

Chuck flipped the paper onto his bed. He would deal with it later, after he reasserted his power. He looked in the mirror, checking his hair. He straightened his collar and turned to leave.

The slam of the door behind him echoed through the hallway. Chuck marched down the hallway to the Pope's office. He yanked open the door. The Pope shuddered as Chuck leaned over the desk, his face inches from the Pope's.

"Who do you think you are?" said Chuck.

"I'm Pope John Paul Georgianringo," the Pope stammered.

"And that means you can blow off god? Just send me to my room?"

The Pope's spine stiffened. He lowered his voice and his lips trembled slightly as he spoke.

"I, I, I," said the Pope.

"You what?"

"I," said the Pope. "wasn't thinking. I'm not used to hosting. The old God only showed up on Christmas and Easter. I apologize."

Chuck backed off slightly, but maintained his dominant position, standing over the Pope.

"That's better," said Chuck. "It's about time you started showing me some respect."

The Pope spread his hands apologetically. Chuck walked behind the desk and leaned over to see what the Pope had been reading. It was a schedule of upcoming events at the Vatican.

"What's this?" Chuck said, pointing at a large event that was being planned.

"The last god," said the Pope. "He's getting married."

"Here?"

The Pope nodded.

"I can cancel it if you want," said the Pope.

Chuck frowned, reading over the plans for God's

wedding. He looked over the guest list, which was quite extensive. He scratched his temple and rubbed his neck. Chuck sighed and put his hand on the Pope's shoulder.

"I don't think so," said Chuck. "Let it go on. But you need to add a name to the guest list."

The Pope nodded and typed Chuck's name at the bottom of the list.

"What are you going to do?"

"What better opportunity do I have," said Chuck. "To introduce myself to my followers?"

Chuck gestured for the Pope to get up.

"Up," he said. "Out of the chair. That's my seat."

The Pope frowned, got up, and shuffled toward the door. He paused at the door.

"Goodbye," said Chuck. The Pope took one last glance then left the office, closing the door behind him.

Chuck sat down and clicked through the recent documents on the Pope's computer. He pulled up a document called 'Stupid Anglicans.' Chuck raised an eyebrow as he read. The Church of England had deployed two agents intent on disrupting God's wedding. Counteragents the Pope had hired had not been heard from since getting the assignment. Worse yet for the Catholics, one of their agents was clearly double-crossing them. He closed his eyes for a moment, considering this new information. He decided to give the Archbishop a call to check in.

"Carl," said Chuck. "It's Chuck. I'm the new god."

Chuck heard a yawn.

"Who?"

"Chuck. The new god."

"What? We have a new god?"

"Yes," said Chuck. "Weren't you informed?"

"No," the Archbishop smacked his lips. "I wasn't. Hold on a sec, willya?"

The Archbishop got himself a drink of water and returned to the phone.

"Sorry about that," he said. "I was asleep. It's the middle of the night you know."

Chuck checked his watch.

"It's 10:30."

"Yeah, like I said. The middle of the night."

"Whatever," said Chuck. "Look, I want to talk to you about the wedding."

"What wedding?"

"God and Sally's wedding."

"Oh yeah," said the Archbishop. "I think I heard about that."

"Of course you did. You're planning on disrupting it."

There was a long pause. Chuck heard the Archbishop take a deep breath.

"Ah, so you know about that," said the Archbishop. "Well, the thing is..."

"Don't worry about it," said Chuck. "I could not care less about that. But I need to tell you: If you ruin the announcement of my reign, I will mess you up."

"What? What announcement?"

"At God's wedding I'm going to announce my reign as god. Do whatever you want to the ceremony. I don't care if God gets married or not. But if you win, when it's over, you'd better pay me the respect I deserve. Got it?"

"Yeah. I got it."

Chuck hung up and leaned back in his chair. That was more like it. That's what being god should be about: Respect. Not paperwork.

At the exact moment the word 'paperwork' passed through his mind, his phone chimed with a text message. Chuck checked his phone and saw some familiar, friendly, and cheerful letters:

Hello, Chuck! We cannot over-emphasize the importance of submitting your reports in a timely manner. If you do not remedy the situation by the extended deadline, substantial penalties may result. Have a nice day!

Chuck deleted the text.

CHAPTER THIRTY-FOUR: BRIGHT, LIGHT, AND FRUITY

Rasputin and Diamondhead crept around the Vatican, with Rasputin careful not to run into the Pope, lest his plan of not going to Church House after all fall apart around him. It didn't occur to them that creeping around actually draws attention, as opposed to just walking around like a normal person. Thankfully, there weren't a ton of normal people walking around the Vatican in any case, so it sort of worked out in an odd way. They fit in by not fitting in.

"We need to make our way to the basement," said Rasputin.

"The basement? Why?" said Diamondhead.

Rasputin tilted his head to one side. That was the first time Diamondhead asked a semi-intelligent question without saying something silly or moronic at the same time.

"Well," said Rasputin. "That's where we'll make our base of operations. That way we won't be found."

"Base?" said Diamondhead. "You mean like a fort? Perfect. I brought plenty of blankets."

Outwardly, Rasputin scowled, but inwardly he smiled. That was the Diamondhead he'd come to know. Rasputin needed that idiocy if Plan 9 was going to succeed. He was depending on it.

Rasputin turned to continue creeping down the hall, when a familiar, comforting smell drew his attention. Coffee. Rich, wonderful coffee. The real thing, not the kind that came free in little crinkly plastic packages in hotels. He approached with intent and Diamondhead followed.

"Welcome to Cafe Wah Gwan Gyal. What can I get for you?"

"I'll have a venti coffee and one of those chocolate pound cake things."

"We don't have venti, we have small, medium, and large."

Rasputin frowned. "You know what I mean."

The teenage girl behind the counter gave Rasputin a withering glare.

"Sorry, I don't speak corporate."

She said 'corporate' as if merely saying the word would somehow, somewhere, result in additional oppression of the proletariat.

Rasputin looked back at Diamondhead to make sure that he hadn't wandered off. Diamondhead looked focused for a change, eager. Rasputin was almost scared, it was so unlike him. Rasputin turned back to the barista.

"OK," said Rasputin. He peered at the barista's name tag. "Allie. I'll play nice. I'll have a large coffee, please."

"Actually, it's Allee´, not Allie," said the barista.

"What?"

"My name is Allee´, not Allie."

"What's the difference?"

"I spell it with two 'e's and an accent mark," she said, pointing to her name tag. "Not with an i-e."

"But it's pronounced the same?"

"Yes."

"Then how can you tell the difference?"

Allee´ shrugged. "I just get a sense when people are saying the i-e instead. I was right, wasn't I?"

Rasputin gestured helplessly. "Can you just give me my cup?"

Allee´ gave him his pound cake and his cup. Rasputin stepped back for Diamondhead to order. Diamondhead stepped up, tapping his fingers on the counter.

"Let's see," he said. "I'll have a grande extra hot, soy, caramel macchiato, no foam, stirred, with whip, extra caramel, at 200 degrees."

"No problem," said Allee´.

Rasputin paid for the drinks, then turned to get his coffee. He considered his options carefully. He inspected the four containers of coffee as Diamondhead sidled up next to him.

"What's going on?" said Diamondhead.

"Trying to pick a coffee."

"It's not that hard really. You just have to get the hang of those little spigots. I tend to shut them off late, spilling coffee. I guess that's why they have those little napkins underneath."

"That's not the problem," Rasputin said. "I like to choose my coffee according to the container that has the description that best matches my mood at the moment."

"Aha," said Diamondhead. "Well, this one is bold, nutty, and juicy."

"I like the bold part, but I'm not feeling nutty and I hope never to feel juicy in my entire life."

"Hmmm. This one is full, bright, and citrus."

"Maybe..."

"Bright, light, and fruity?"

"Definitely not."

"Last choice: rich, smoky, and smooth."

"I guess, maybe. I like the rich part and I'm definitely feeling smooth at the moment."

"Smooth, really?"

135

Rasputin shot Diamondhead a glare. "Yes, really. I'm not sure about smoky. Maybe. I have been sneaking around a lot, kind of like the smoke monster from *Lost*."

"The smoke monster didn't sneak around."

"Yes, it did."

"No, it didn't," said Diamondhead. "There was that horn or siren or whatever that always went off right before the smoke monster came. Unless you start sounding a horn everywhere you go, there's no comparison."

Rasputin couldn't believe it. Diamondhead had gotten the better of him in an argument. He sighed and rubbed his temples.

"Fine," said Rasputin. "I'll have the full, bright, and citrus."

Diamondhead filled Rasputin's cup for him.

"Here you go," he said. "One cup of Capital Blend. Whatever that means."

pretentious. Wait, that's redundant. It just sounds French."

"It is French."

"I know that," said Rasputin. "But you shouldn't use French unless you're from France. It's pretentious."

"Yeah, but the word climax is unseemly."

"How so?"

"You know," said Diamondhead, squirming uncomfortably. "Men. Women. Climax."

Rasputin rolled his eyes. "Please. It's not unseemly. But denouement is definitely pretentious. People that say denouement ought to shampoo my crotch."

Diamondhead cocked his head to one side.

"You want somebody to shampoo your crotch?"

"What?" said Rasputin. "Of course not."

"But you just said-"

"I know what I said."

"So what does that even mean?"

"It's an expression."

"No it's not, I've never heard that before in my life."

"Sure it is," said Rasputin. "Jack Nicholson used it in *As Good As It Gets*."

Now Diamondhead rolled his eyes.

"Even if he did, that doesn't make it an expression. It's a movie. Plus, he's Jack Nicholson. You're not."

"So?"

"So you never banged Lara Flynn Boyle and you can't use that 'expression.'"

"Wait a second," said Rasputin. "Jack Nicholson slept with Lara Flynn Boyle?"

"Yeah, you didn't know that?"

"No, man, that's gross."

"Yeah, I know, she's all skin and bones. Like having sex with a mummy."

"No, I meant Jack Nicholson. He's an old man."

"I'm not gay or anything, but I'd rather sleep with Jack Nicholson than Lara Flynn Boyle," Diamondhead said.

Rasputin just stared at Diamondhead blankly.

"What's the matter?" said Diamondhead. "Can't handle the truth?"

That was too much for Rasputin - being out-Nicholsoned by Diamondhead was more than he could bear. He stormed toward the door.

"Get it ready," he commanded. "When I get back, we'll finish our prep for Plan 9. Be ready."

Diamondhead wondered to himself what it was he was supposed to get ready. He had only a dim understanding of what they were trying to do. He thought back to the blank pieces of paper the Pope had given him and couldn't reconcile them with what Rasputin was having them do. Of course, the Pope's main bit of direction to them had been to not eat green beans, so his briefing may not have been as helpful as he might have liked. As it was, Diamondhead did the best he could to ready himself, given that he had no idea what they were doing, nor how long Rasputin would be gone. He checked his pockets, making sure he still had his wallet, keys, and a pen. That confirmed, he sat back and decided to take a quick nap while he had the opportunity. Soon, he was snoring, his feet up, head back. This was one of Diamondhead's principle talents: The uncanny ability to nap just about anywhere.

His nap was interrupted as Rasputin stormed back into the room. He glared at Diamondhead and got to work. Diamondhead yawned, stretched, and walked over to Rasputin. He stood watching for awhile.

"So," said Diamondhead. "Whatcha doing?"

"I'm attaching these electrodes to all the crypts."

"Oh, yeah."

Diamondhead stood idly by. He picked up his coffee and took a loud slurp. He tapped his toe and hummed absently. Rasputin shut his eyes for a moment, trying to tune Diamondhead out. Rasputin wasn't sure, but he thought the tune Diamondhead was humming was Copa Cabana. Now that was going to be in his head the entire day. Finally he gave up and turned around to face Diamondhead.

"Do you mind? That's quite annoying."

"Sorry," said Diamondhead. "It's just something to do, you know?"

"You could try being helpful."

"Sure, sure," said Diamondhead. "I'd love to help. What do you need me to do?"

"There are a lot of crypts. You could help put these electrodes up."

"Sure."

Diamondhead started putting up the electrodes, again humming as he did so.

"So what's this for?" he said. "These crypts don't seem to be electrical or anything. Oh! Are we putting up Christmas lights?"

"No," said Rasputin. "We are not putting up Christmas lights. For one thing, it isn't Christmastime. It's June. For another thing, you would not put up Christmas lights in the catacombs. Crypts are not for decoration."

"So, what then?"

"Plan 9."

"That's an answer without an answer."

"Yeah, well."

Rasputin and Diamondhead went on working in silence. Soon, they finished attaching the electrodes to all the crypts throughout the catacombs. Rasputin strung them together to a master switch. Diamondhead looked on in interest.

"So what's the switch for?"

Rasputin sighed and sat down, sweat pouring off of him.

"It will activate Plan 9, when the time comes."

"And when is that?"

"A little over a week," said Rasputin. "At God's wedding. It'll be spectacular."

"What, exactly, will be spectacular?"

"Let me ask you this: Have you ever wanted to meet Vincent Price?"

"Yeah, sure. I guess."

"Just you wait then."

CHAPTER THIRTY-SEVEN: HOW HARD COULD IT BE?

Sally was smiling broadly, having a wonderful time. God was not. It wasn't that he didn't enjoy dancing, it was that they were not so much learning to dance as they were learning a complicated series of choreographed moves that seemed intended to make him appear as foolish as possible. The instructor, Chaz Michaels, kept telling him to watch his frame, whatever that was supposed to mean. The fact that Chaz only had the best things to say about Sally's performance didn't make things any easier.

"Frame!" said Chaz, hitting God in the elbow. "Watch your frame."

God glared at Chaz, then looked back at Sally and gave a weak smile.

"You owe me big for this," he said.

"No, I don't," said Sally. "You owe me big from leaving me at the concert, remember? This is just payback. Now remember to smile, dear. You're supposed to be having a fantastic time dancing with the woman of your dreams. Act like it."

"I am dancing with the woman of my dreams," he said.

"But the dream didn't include some other guy hitting me in the elbow every five seconds, telling me to fix my frame. I never had any complaints about my frame until now."

Sally laughed and sat down as Chaz worked with God alone for awhile. God looked completely humiliated as he danced with Chaz. The humiliation wasn't from dancing with another man. It was from dancing with another man so poorly. Chaz, for his part, did not look any happier dancing with God. After a few minutes, Chaz excused himself, needing to leave the room to vent some frustration before continuing. As Chaz left, muttering to himself, God sat down next to Sally.

"He seems pretty mad," said God.

"Yeah, you really stumped him, I think."

God took a deep breath and took Sally's hand.

"I'm really trying, you know."

"I know," said Sally. "But the waltz doesn't seem to be your thing."

"I blame marching band," said God. "It programmed me to count to four, not to three."

"You were in marching band?"

"Yeah," said God. "I played trombone."

"Why did you pick the trombone?"

"Because," said God. "It's the only instrument with a slide. No valves, buttons, or any of that crap."

"What about the F attachment?"

God dismissed the thought with a wave of his hand.

"Never used one, never will. Valves do not belong on a trombone. Trombone players that use F attachments are just lazy. You don't really need one, you know. You can play any note you need on a standard slide. Sure, sometimes it's hard, since you have to move the slide all the way out, from all the way in, in between two notes, but that's the challenge of the trombone. The F attachment is just cheating."

"But aren't there valve trombones too, that don't use a slide?"

"Don't get me started. Valve trombones are nothing but glorified trumpets. They aren't really trombones at all."

Chaz came back in, looking a little less harried. He looked at God, gave a half-smile, then turned to Sally.

"Let's put the finishing touches on your part, my dear," he said. "In the last few minutes of the lesson. We'll pick up again with the gentleman tomorrow. I promise you, we will whip him into shape in time for the wedding."

Sally took his hand and she and Chaz worked through the routine a couple more times before the lesson was over. God was relieved and watched with interest as Sally waltzed around the dance floor. She was really quite talented. He wanted to be a better dancer for her, but he wasn't sure it was in the cards. He would give it all he had.

Chaz and Sally finished, and she came over to God. Chaz left without saying goodbye. God didn't blame him.

"Are you ready to go?" said Sally.

"Sure, let's go home."

"No, not home," said Sally. "At least not for long. Don't you remember? We're having dinner with my mother tonight. She wanted to meet you before the wedding. I think she wants to look you over and see if she approves."

God's face fell. He'd forgotten all about meeting Sally's mother. He wasn't anxious to meet her, since Sally's descriptions of her had been less than complimentary. He threw his hands in the air and sighed heavily.

"OK," he said. "When and where again? What should I wear?"

"Anything is fine. Don't worry. You don't need to impress my mother. I don't care if she approves or not."

God gave Sally a look that said he wasn't nearly dumb enough to believe her, but that he appreciated her effort to make him feel better.

"OK," she said. "Put on your blue shirt. It makes you look respectable. We're supposed to meet her in about an hour at the restaurant. We have time to stop home for you to change. But really, it doesn't matter. She'll love you because I love you."

God smiled and grasped Sally's hand in his. He leaned toward her and gave her a gentle kiss on the cheek. She took his arm as they walked to the car. Once they had arrived home, God put on his blue shirt, as Sally had said. He examined his hair critically in the mirror. His hair was short, so there was little he could do with it, but he still felt vaguely dissatisfied with it. Sally came up behind him and slipped her arms around his waist. God smiled and put his arm around her. He fussed with his hair one more time before they got back in the car to go to the restaurant.

God and Sally found a table. The waitress took their drink order and God began to hope that Sally's mother simply wouldn't show. Maybe she would pass by a circus and decide to go there instead. Something. Anything. He wrapped his napkin around his finger and unwrapped it. He toyed with his silverware and forced a smile as Sally reached across the table to put her hand on his.

After a few minutes, Sally's mother arrived, able to resist the lure of the circus after all. Sally smiled and waved her over to the table. Sally hugged her mom, who then glanced at God uncomfortably. God stood up, couldn't decide whether to offer a handshake or a hug, and got caught in no man's land. Sally's mom offered her hand and God shook it with a grim smile.

"Nice to meet you," she said. "I'm Louise."

"It's nice to meet you as well," God said. "I'm God."

Louise sat down across from God, who was fiddling with his napkin. Louise wore her dress like a uniform. The functional gray outfit had no flourish, no pop of color, no spontaneity. God fidgeted, wishing he had been able to get his hair cut before meeting Louise.

"I'm so glad we all could get together before the wedding," said Sally. "I was happy to hear you could fly in early."

"Me too," said Louise. "I need to make sure my little

girl is in good hands."

"Oh mom," said Sally. "I'm thirty years old! You don't need to worry about me any more."

"Mother's always worry, dear. It's our job. Even when you're thirty. How did you two meet? Sally hasn't hardly told me a thing."

"Mom! I told you I was seeing someone."

"Yes, but you were always light on the details."

"We met at the airport," said God. "When Sally was leaving for her Wheel of Fortune trip. She just bowled me over. It took me awhile to win her over."

"Not really," said Sally. "I knew you were something special right away. Maybe not always in a good way, but special for sure."

"Thanks, sweetie."

Louise gave a wan smile and cleared her throat.

"So, God, what brought you to Jamaica?"

"Sally did. I knew she won a trip here and I had to see her again. I waited at the airport every day until one day she fell out of the sky. I ran into her when I went to get lunch. I've been at her side ever since."

"It was meant to be," said Sally.

"You just flew to Jamaica and stalked her at the airport until she showed up?"

Louise turned to her daughter.

"Doesn't that seem odd to you?"

"It's not like that," said God. "I love her. Ever since I first met her. She has a quality. I even retired so I could be with her."

"Wait a minute" said Louise. "You don't have a job?"

"No, like I said, I'm retired."

"So what do you do for money? I want to be sure my girl is well-supported."

"Usually I just point to where it says 'In God We Trust' on the money and ask for a line of credit."

"So you just roll up more and more debt?"

Louise looked at Sally worriedly.

"Are you comfortable with that?"

"Mom, really. What century do you think this is? God doesn't need to support me. I can support the both of us."

Louise gave a cold smile and put her hand on Sally's.

"My dear, I'm afraid you can't even support yourself on your salary. I'm not sure what a PR specialist makes, but it can't be that much. Especially after taking your time graduating. Most people your age would have a graduate degree. If only you hadn't spent all that time wandering around Europe."

Sally shrugged and looked at God. He looked around, desperate for help. None was available and God floundered.

"I also have a rock band," God said hopefully. "Trinity."

"I think I've heard of you," said Louise. "Didn't you just break up? Your lead guitarist left, didn't he? What was his name again? Jose?"

"Jesus." said God.

"Right," said Louise. "Jesus. Didn't he leave the group?"

God's face fell.

"Yeah," God admitted. "But Trinity is still together. The Holy Ghost and I."

"Come now," Louise said. "You can't have a trinity with just two members."

"That's true," God said. "I guess."

"Mom, it'll be fine," Sally said. "He takes good care of me. We have a nice house, a car, and everything."

Louise shook her head and looked as if tears were forming in her eyes.

"I just don't know," Louise said. "I don't think I can support you marrying a man who can't provide for you. " She sighed. "I just want the best for you, sweetheart."

"Mom..." Sally began.

"No, it's OK," said God. "I understand her point. It's not a problem. The wedding isn't until Saturday. That gives me five days to find a job. If I find a job before the wedding, you'll give us your blessing, won't you?"

"Sure," said Louise. "But you have to be employed by then."

"Not to worry," said God. "I will find a job. How hard could it be?"

CHAPTER THIRTY-EIGHT: SOMETIMES YOU HAVE TO JUST LET IT GO

Thor, Frank, and Josh Ua were moving through the line at the Golden Corral. Thor frowned as he inspected the food in the buffet. He leaned over, sniffed the macaroni and cheese, then scooped some up and let it drip back into the pan. He turned to Josh Ua.

"When you said we'd discuss what you wanted over a bite to eat, this is not exactly what I had in mind."

"Well I love it," said Frank. "It's all you can eat and I can eat a lot. Especially of this stuff."

Frank piled half his plate with chocolate pudding with fried chicken occupying the other half. He grabbed a second plate and started loading up on mashed potatoes. Thor looked on in disgust. He half-heartedly took some grilled chicken and applesauce, and looked around for a table. Ua was already sitting down and eating speedily.

"Thanks for waiting," said Thor as he sat across from Joshua Ua.

He ignored Thor and continued to eat. Frank sat down and started eating as well. Thor was disgusted. They had poor manners even by Viking standards. Thor ate lightly. The food did not really appeal to him and he had lost his appetite as a result of Josh and Frank's behavior. Finally the two of them stopped shoveling food into their mouths and the conversation could finally begin. Truly, Thor could not care less, but Frank had been insistent that they find out why Ua had bailed them out. Frank looked at Ua expectantly.

"Man, I don't care what you say," said Ua. "Those ribs were as good as you'll get anywhere. Why pay three times the price when you don't have to?"

"Yeah, it's great, especially for the money," said Frank. He sat back and belched appreciatively. "So, why did you bail us out?"

"I have a job for you."

"What kind of job? Does it pay well? Ooh, ooh, is it Chairman of the Federal Reserve? I am an accountant, you know."

"I was just about to tell you. But no, it is not Chairman of the Federal Reserve."

"Oh, sorry. I've never been bailed out of jail by a mysterious stranger before. It's exciting. And when I get excited, I talk a lot. Some people say it's because my mother was chatty when she was little, but I'm not sure what that would have to do with it. Maybe if it had been my dad, sure, but why would I inherit something like that from my mother? Not that I don't have anything in common with my mother, it just seems a lot less likely. Besides, it's not like hair color or something. Can you really inherit excessive chattiness? I mean,-"

"So the job I have for you," Josh Ua interrupted. "Is to counteract an Anglican plot against the Catholic Church. We don't have a lot of time, less than a week now."

"Less than a week until what?"

"Until the Anglicans begin Plan 9."

"OK, so what's Plan 9?"

"Their plot against the Catholics."

"Right," said Frank. "And why do we care about that? Are you Catholic?"

"No," said Ua. "I'm an atheist."

"That's too bad."

"Why is that?"

"Because God exists. He visited my house."

"Really?"

"Yeah," Frank said. "I've been looking for him ever since. Plus, if you haven't noticed, the guy sitting across from you is the Scandinavian god of thunder."

Thor smiled and nodded, not really listening. He was mostly drinking his root beer and scoping out the dining room for chicks. The pickings were slim.

"Not only that," Frank said. "But God just played a concert, the very one from which we were arrested."

"The Trinity concert?" Ua asked.

"Yeah."

"I thought that was just a gimmick. You know, like The Police. They aren't really police."

"True. That would be something, wouldn't it? It would be really embarrassing to be arrested by Sting," said Frank. "But Trinity's the real deal."

"Even so," Ua said. "I'm definitely not Catholic."

"So why get involved at all?"

Josh was temporarily distracted by Thor winking at a woman seated across the restaurant. She averted her eyes and Thor moved on.

"I'm sorry, what did you say?"

"Why get involved if you aren't even Catholic?"

"I owe someone a favor and this is paying it back."

"Could you be any more vague?"

"Sure," Ua said. "I'm getting involved for good reasons, known only to me."

Frank winced. He'd forgotten about Ua's complete humorlessness. He looked at Thor for some commiseration, but he was still on the hunt for a female companion. Thor was faring quite poorly, which surprised

Frank. He would have assumed that Thor, being a rather well-built god, would have an easier time with the ladies. Maybe it was just the Golden Corral crowd, but Thor was striking out left and right, like he was a one-man personification of the Pittsburgh Pirates.

"So then, what's the plan?"

"Ours or theirs?"

"Either one," said Frank. "I'm still not sure I grasp exactly what you want us to do. Or what the Anglicans are doing. Or what the point of it all is."

"OK, I get it," said Joshua Ua. "Here's the deal. The Anglicans have declared a Holy War against the Catholics. They have sent two agents to the Vatican, who have been working in the catacombs below the Vatican preparing for Plan 9. It isn't clear what they hope to accomplish, but the word on the street is that they are planning to stop God's wedding this weekend."

"Word on the street? Who exactly told you this?"

"A barista named Allee´ that works in the Vatican. One of the agents told her of their plan. He really likes his soy caramel macchiatos. He didn't seem to know any other details though. I think it was probably the Catholic agent that the Anglican agents appear to have turned."

"We're going on the word of a coffeehouse worker named Ally?"

"Her name is Allee´, with two e's and an accent mark. Not a y."

"But it's pronounced the same."

"Yes."

Frank decided to let it go. Thor, meanwhile, was chatting up a woman who had walked by with a tray of spaghetti. He leaned over to Frank and Josh.

"Hey guys, you want to go to a party later? She wants to get together, but she needs dates for her friends too. You in?"

Josh and Frank glanced at each other, then looked back at Thor.

"No," they said in unison. Thor grimaced and turned back toward the woman, spreading his hands apologetically.

"So assuming this Allee´ is right, what do we need to do?" said Frank.

"Well, I'm not entirely sure," said Ua. "That's one reason I bailed you guys out - I definitely need some help figuring this out. It also helps that you guys can get into God's wedding this weekend, whereas I'm not invited."

"What are you talking about? I don't remember getting invited to God's wedding."

"Technically, you weren't," said Josh. "But Thor was. They invited all the retired gods that hang out at Giovanni's."

"What?" said Frank. "Thor!"

Thor turned to Frank, no longer distracted by women.

"What is it?" said Thor. "Are we done yet? This place sucks. It's like a sausage festival, but not the good kind of sausage festival."

"Focus. We're almost done," said Frank. "Were you invited to God's wedding?"

"Yeah, sure," said Thor. "He invited everyone from the bar. I'm not going."

"What? Why not?"

"Why would I?" said Thor. "It's not like we are buddies or anything. Now there's some rule that I have to go the wedding of everyone that drinks Bud Lite?"

"We don't have time for that," said Ua. "We can only go to one wedding. It needs to be God's wedding or the plan won't work."

Thor and Frank let it pass.

"Well, technically, I didn't even RSVP," said Thor. "I guess I could go. At least there'll be an open bar."

"Yeah," said Frank. "Plus, there'll be fighting. Your two favorite things."

"Who will we be fighting?" said Thor.

"The Anglicans," said Ua. "Weren't you paying

attention?"

"No," said Thor. "I wasn't. Anglicans, eh? Nice. I never cared for the Anglicans anyway."

"Why not?" said Frank.

"I don't know. They just seem like a pansy religion. They only started in the first place so some king could get divorced. What do you think of that? Pansy or what?"

"I don't know," said Frank. "Would a pansy found a religion to get divorced? I admit, it's an odd way to begin, but I wouldn't say pansy."

"Whatever," said Thor. "In any case, if there'll be drinking and fighting, I'm there."

"And vice-versa," said Frank.

"Good," said Ua. "So you're both in. Frank, I won't be able to attend, so I'll have to rely on you to figure out what the Anglicans are up to and foil their plans."

"Did you just say 'foil their plans'?"

"Yes. Why?"

"Nobody says foil. Unless you're the villain in a James Bond movie."

"But I do want you to foil their plans."

"Yeah," said Frank. "It's OK, you can't help it."

"Help what?"

"Being you."

Joshua Ua nodded. "I know what you mean."

CHAPTER THIRTY-NINE: WORKING FOR THE WEEKEND

God paced in the reception area as he read over his resume for the thousandth time. He had never been on a job interview before and the stakes couldn't be higher. He only had three days until the wedding and he needed to get a job or risk having the whole thing called off. He had been able to get some interviews arranged quickly. Now he just had to make them pay off. He was dressed in a suit that Sally had picked out for him and she had helped him hastily put together his resume. He tapped his toes nervously until a young man wearing khakis and a bright red polo shirt came out to greet him. God looked at him uncertainly. He was expecting someone older.

"Hi, I'm Chris," said the interviewer. "You must be God."

"That's right," God said as he extended his hand. "Nice to meet you."

Chris led God to a meeting room and the two of them sat down around a clear glass table. The chair had been raised up as far as it would go and God struggled briefly to adjust it.

"Sorry about that, the cleaning crew does that every night. No one know why," said Chris, who had successfully adjusted his own chair. "So, God, tell me about yourself."

Chris peered over God's resume as God fidgeted in his seat before answering.

"In my most recent position, I oversaw around two billion Christians worldwide. Mostly in Europe and the Americas."

Chris whipped out a pen and began to take notes on God's resume.

"And what were your responsibilities there?"

"Responsibilities?"

"Yeah, what did you do, you know, day to day?"

God rubbed his hands together, resisting the urge to crack his knuckles.

"I would listen to people's prayers, you know, and give comfort to the grieving. I'd influence the outcomes of the Super Bowl and other major sporting events."

"I've often wondered about that," said Chris. "So you're the God athletes are always thanking?"

God smiled and nodded.

"Yep, that's me," God said. "Though to be honest, I usually favored the more prepared, talented team. I'm not really sure it made that much difference in the end."

"So what results did you drive?"

"What?"

"What were the results of what you did? We're very results-driven here. Look."

Chris took a laminated document out of his folder and handed it to God.

"Being results-driven is eleventh on our list of corporate values."

"Out of fifteen," God said, looking over the document. "Just above being enthusiastic and just below delivering WOW."

"They aren't really ranked. That is just the order in

which we list them."

"Ah, I see."

God pretended to read the list as he gathered his thoughts.

"Hmm. Let's see. The Steelers won the Super Bowl a bunch of times. Five or six maybe."

"Not football results, the results of what you did," said Chris. "How many prayers you answered, widows you comforted, you know, stuff like that. Your customer service metrics."

"I didn't think to keep track," said God. "I was never too big on the answering of prayers. I mostly just listened. More like a counselor than a customer service rep."

"I see. What did you make there?"

"I didn't make anything. Like I said, I listened to prayers and such."

"No, no, I mean your salary. What were you paid?"

"Paid? I wasn't paid."

Chris frowned and put his pen up to his lips.

"You weren't paid. So it was a volunteer position?"

"I suppose you could say that," God said. "The perks were good. Do those count?"

"No. I'm afraid not," Chris frowned. "Do you have any real experience?"

"That isn't real experience?"

"I mean paid experience," said Chris. "Did you have a job prior to your position as god?"

"Oh, yeah, I worked at Sears."

"The department store?"

"Well, no. Elijah Sears, a merchant in Hebron. I worked for him selling myrrh. I always received excellent customer satisfaction scores there. Admittedly, my sales were weak, but I think that was because no one really knew what to do with myrrh."

Chris shook his head as he flipped over God's resume, finding just the one page after all.

"Do you have any references? If I called this Elijah,

what would he tell me?" said Chris.

"That was a long time ago. I think Elijah has been dead for around two thousand years."

"What about for your position as god? Who did you report to there?"

God frowned and squirmed in his seat. His tie was bothering him and all of a sudden it felt like his jacket was one size too small. He felt like the interview was slipping out of his control. The poor guy didn't even realize that he never had the interview under control to begin with.

"I didn't really report to anyone. I was god for crying out loud. I have the new god's phone number, if that would help."

"Can he speak to your job performance?"

"I'm afraid not."

Chris sat back and rubbed his temples.

"I'm really sorry, God, but I don't think you'd be a good fit here. We're looking for someone with more experience."

"But I've got over 2000 years of experience!"

"Paid experience," said Chris. "Relevant to the position."

Chris got up and opened the door for God.

"Good luck," he said.

"Thanks," said God. "I guess."

God shuffled out of the building, distraught. His other interviews that day followed the same pattern. Getting a job in less than a week was going to be more challenging than he had thought. He went home and started preparing for the next day's interviews. He only had two days left. He needed to make them count.

CHAPTER FORTY: VATICAN HOT DOGS ARE THE BEST

The Pope crept to the door of his office. He cracked it open slightly and peered inside. Chuck glared at him from behind the desk. The Pope poked his head inside and coughed slightly.

"What is it?" said Chuck.

"I'm sorry, but are you going to be using my office all night?"

"What if I say yes? What of it?"

"That's fine," said the Pope. "I was just wondering."

Chuck got up and walked to the door. He shook his head as he looked the Pope up and down.

"I'm a little disappointed in you. You've got no fight. I come in here and you just rolled over like an itchy dog, folded like a cheap suit."

The Pope nodded morosely.

"OK, I get it."

"You let me walk all over you like a cheap doormat."

"I said I get it."

"You were a bigger pushover than Glass Joe."

"That's enough! I get it! I get it!"

The Pope shut the door, leaving Chuck alone in the office, which was just as well, because Chuck couldn't think of any more ways to insultingly describe the Pope's behavior. Sure, he could've said that the Pope folded like a lawn chair, but that would be re-using the word 'folded' and Chuck didn't play that way. He was just pleased that he was able to work in a *Punch Out!* reference and was hopeful that it wouldn't be lost on the Pope, or anyone else that might hear of the event later, either in person, or in some sort of text-based account of the event. Chuck went back to reviewing the documents on the Pope's computer. There was nothing else that interesting, just a bunch of draft letters to the editor of *Teen People*.

Chuck left the office. The Pope was nowhere in sight. Chuck shrugged and walked toward the main entrance. He didn't care about the Pope; he cared about food. His stomach rumbled. He had noticed a hot dog cart outside earlier. It was nearly 3 A.M., but he figured that would just mean there would be no line.

Chuck left the Vatican and looked around in vain for a hot dog cart. He walked the streets, looking for any sign of hot dogs, or maybe a gyro cart if one happened to appear first. Gyros weren't a perfect substitute for hot dogs by any stretch, but sometimes you have to work with what you've got. Not finding anything, he gave up and walked back toward the Vatican.

Naturally, on the other side of the Vatican, only feet from where he began, were two hot dog stands. Even more predictably, there were lines at both. He got in line at the stand that had slightly fewer people in line and waited impatiently.

A man dressed in a knit cap, plus hunter's cap, approached him. Chuck tried to avoid eye contact with the man, who was dressed as though it was winter, when in fact it was quite warm out. Unfortunately, like many strange people, the man had a preternatural skill for ferreting out eye contact despite Chuck's best efforts and thus paving the way for a conversation.

"Sir!" the man said. "Would you like to donate to the homeless?"

"Sorry," said Chuck. "I don't have any cash on me."

Chuck looked away and hoped fervently that the man would move on without noticing the bill he was now handing the hot dog vendor and the change that was being returned to him. Chuck was halfway lucky. The man seemed not to have noticed the cash, but did not seem like he was giving moving on much consideration.

"There are a lot of homeless in this city, you know," said the man.

Chuck looked him over again and wondered whether the man himself was one of them.

"That's a shame," said Chuck. "But I really must be going."

The man managed to get in Chuck's way while appearing as though he was trying to get out of Chuck's way. Chuck ended up standing there, facing the man again, as if he intended the conversation to continue. Really, Chuck just wanted to enjoy his hot dog in peace.

"Any small donation would be much appreciated, sir."

"I understand that," Chuck said. "But as I said, I simply don't have any cash on hand. One of the downsides of the coming cashless society, I'm sure."

The man frowned, then looked back at the hot dog cart.

"Didn't you just buy a hot dog?"

Chuck glanced at the hot dog in his hand.

"No."

"Then why were you in line at a hot dog stand?" The man asked. "And where did you get that hot dog?"

"OK, Sherlock, you got me," said Chuck. "I bought a hot dog. So what?"

"So you must have cash."

Chuck was mildly surprised. He hadn't expected the man to be able to put two and two together. At least not and come up with four. Portland, Oregon, maybe, but not four.

"OK, if it'll make you feel better, I do have cash," said Chuck. "But I'm still not going to donate anything."

"Why not?" said the man. "Don't you care about the homeless?"

"Not really," said Chuck, scratching at his armpit. "At least, not that much. Besides, if I did care about the homeless, I still wouldn't give you any money. What kind of person goes out fundraising at hot dog stands at three in the morning? Are you raising money to send the homeless to raves or what? That's just weird."

Chuck tried to take a bite of his hot dog, but the wrapper wasn't pulled back far enough, plus it had some of that plastic wrap inside the wrapper, which was in the way too. Of course it made perfect sense to sell hermetically sealed hot dogs outside the Vatican at three in the morning. Chuck's face reddened as he struggled with the wrapper.

"I'm sorry," he said. "But I've got to go."

Chuck went back into the Vatican, not even pausing to put ketchup on his hot dog. Even so, he wolfed down the hot dog quickly and it tasted fantastic. He briefly considered venturing back out for another, but didn't feel up to another confrontation with Mr. Help-The-Homeless-At-Three-In-The-Morning.

Chuck paused on his way back to his room to check out the Vatican's event calendar again. He wanted to be sure of when God's wedding was scheduled. He had a few questions about the dental plan and he wasn't sure when the *Highway to Heaven* requirement kicked in. Or, for that matter, who he would have to answer to if he didn't want to watch Michael Landon smile angelically as he saves cancer-stricken war widows from evil capitalists that are planning on evicting them from their childhood homes to build a factory that is powered by kittens and produces cigarette-smoking machine guns.

CHAPTER FORTY-ONE: IT'S THE SHIPPING THAT GETS YOU

God meandered toward the car. He was tired at the end of another long day of job hunting. It was two days before the wedding and he had nothing. No leads, no interviews, and certainly no job. God drove toward the Vatican, hoping to speak with the Pope. After all the help God had given the Pope over the years, he figured the Pope could return the favor just this once. After all, God had gotten Suzy Stephenson to go with the Pope to his high school prom. God was pretty sure the Pope had made it to second base with Suzy that night and second base with Suzy was better than getting to third base with many women.

God approached the Vatican, intent on finding the Pope. On the stairs outside, a man dressed in an inferior-quality suit of armor sat, lines across his brow, dejected. The knight tapped his fingers against his armor, which would have been annoying except the man looked too pathetic to be annoying. God approached the knight and sat next to him on the steps.

"Hey man," said God. "What's going on?"

The man glanced up at God, with tears forming in his eyes. He wiped his eyes, shook his head, and looked down at his feet. He sobbed softly and God patted him on the back.

"Come on, man, pull it together. It'll all be OK."

"How do you know?"

"Well, I'm God, for one thing."

The knight wiped the tears from his eyes and gathered himself together. A slight, hopeful smile flashed across his face.

"Yeah? You're God?"

"Sort of," he said. "I retired, so now it's just my name. But I was, until a few weeks ago."

"So can you see the future?"

"No."

"So how do you know it'll all be OK?"

"Because," said God. "That's one of the things they tell you when you become God. That no matter how badly you think you might screw things up, it'll all be OK."

"Who is they?"

"You know, they," said God, shrugging. "Trust me. After all, it says 'In God We Trust' right here."

God flipped the knight a quarter. The knight caught it and rubbed it between his fingers. He looked back up at God.

"Thanks."

"No problem. What has you so down?"

"I've been looking for something for a long time and have never found it."

"Inner peace?"

"No," said the knight, smiling. "I found that ages ago. I gave it up when I started searching for the Sampo."

"Sampo? What is that?"

"I don't know," said the knight. "That's part of the problem."

"So why are you looking for it?"

"I don't really remember. It seemed like a good idea at

the time. Some Finnish guy I met once kept going on and on about it. I guess I just got caught up in the excitement."

God frowned, then got to his feet.

"OK, come with me, we're getting to the bottom of this."

God gestured for the man to follow him and they made their way to the Pope's office. The Pope wasn't there and God sat in the Pope's chair and turned on the computer. God went to Google and typed in Sampo. He turned the screen towards the knight.

"There you go. You can buy a Sampo lock snap swivel for twenty-five dollars from Amazon. Plus shipping."

The knight stood with his mouth agape, staring at the screen.

"You should have really started with Google in the first place," said God. "It almost always works. Except for this one time I was trying to find a particular bottle of soy sauce. I tried everything, even taking a picture of the bottle and using it to search, but got nothing. Apparently Google falls down when it comes to Asian condiments for some reason."

The knight nodded and sat down slowly into a chair.

"I can't believe it," he said. "So many years wasted."

"Don't take it so hard. After all, did you really have anything better to do than travel the world? If you hadn't done this, you probably would've wasted your life trying to help Facebook come up with a more efficient method for displaying advertisements for Old Spice."

"I guess."

"Besides," said God. "No matter how much you think you screwed up, it'll all be OK."

The knight smiled and extended his hand. God shook it and smiled back.

"Thanks for everything."

The knight left and God waited alone in the Pope's office. It was pretty bare, all in all. A few papers on the desk next to the computer, the two chairs, and a refrigerator filled with V8 occupied the entire office. The Pope didn't seem to be the sentimental sort, since there were no personal items around. No pictures, diplomas, awards, or anything like that. The only thing that was even close to personal was a Pope-shaped squeaky toy that God assumed someone had given the Pope as a gag. After a few minutes, the door opened and the Pope entered. He threw his big hat on his desk and slumped in his chair, sighing loudly. He remained with his eyes closed for a few moments, until God cleared his throat.

"Oh! Sorry, I didn't know anyone was here," said the Pope.

"It's my fault, I let myself in. I needed to Google something, so I borrowed your computer. I hope you don't mind."

"Not at all. As long as you weren't looking for pornography."

The Pope laughed and God chuckled along with him.

"Seriously though," said the Pope. "You weren't looking for porn?"

"No," God said. "I was just trying to track down a Sampo for a friend. Found one on Amazon for twenty-five dollars."

"Including shipping?"

"No, that's six dollars extra, unless you're an Amazon Prime member."

"Not a bad price, but six bucks for shipping? Come on."

The Pope drummed his fingers on his desk and looked at God expectantly.

"So," the Pope said. "What brings you here exactly?"

"I'm supposed to get married here in a couple of days," said God. "And I have a bit of a problem."

"Cardinal Tito usually handles weddings. I don't really get involved personally."

"No, no, it isn't anything to do with the arrangements here. Everything is going fine with all that."

God hoped to himself that it was actually true. He hadn't bothered asking Sally if there were any last-minute details that needed clearing up.

"You see," God continued. "My fiancé's mother won't give us her blessing unless I have a job before the wedding. I was hoping you could help. I've been on a bunch of interviews, but no luck."

"I see. You want me to excommunicate the people that refused to hire you. Consider it done."

"No, that's not it. I don't need you to excommunicate my interviewers."

"You want me to excommunicate her mother? Done!"

"No," said God. "I don't want anyone excommunicated."

The Pope frowned and drummed his fingers on his desk again. He sat back in his chair, grabbed a strip of beef jerky off of a shelf, and offered it to God. God shook his head and the Pope took a bite from the jerky, thinking.

"You don't want anyone excommunicated?"

"No."

"Are you sure? I've never excommunicated anybody and it's on my bucket list. I really don't mind."

"Sorry, I'm quite sure."

"OK, fine," the Pope pouted. "So what do you want then?"

"A job. Like I said, I need to get a job before the wedding."

"Ah. But isn't being god your job?"

"It was, but I retired a few weeks ago."

"Really."

"Yes, I would have thought you would have known by now. Hasn't Chuck been by yet?"

"Chuck? Oh yes, now that you mention it. I still can't believe our Lord and Savior's name is Chuck. It's going to take some getting used to."

The Pope sighed and took another bite of beef jerky. It was a lot to take in, plus this was usually the Pope's nap time. The Pope checked his watch, then buzzed his secretary and asked for Cardinal Jermaine. Moments later Jermaine appeared in the doorway.

"Yes, sir?" said Jermaine.

"God needs a job. Can we do something for him? Maybe your assistant?"

"Yes, sir. Very good."

Jermaine turned to God.

"I look forward to working with you."

God nodded and Jermaine left the room. The Pope smiled and dug into his mini-fridge. He emerged with two cans of V8 and handed one to God. The Pope smiled and raised his can in the air.

"To celebrate," said the Pope.

"No thanks," said God. "I hate V8."

The Pope's smile disappeared. He took a drink from his V8 and set it down.

"You hate V8?"

"Yeah," said God. "Sorry, there's just something about vegetable juice that is somehow unsettling. Maybe it's the color. It's too much like drinking blood."

The Pope pursed his lips.

"It's very nutritious," he said. "And delicious."

"It's fine if you like V8, it just isn't my thing."

The Pope sighed and looked toward the ceiling. He ran his fingers through his hair and sighed again, audibly. He looked back toward God.

"I'm sorry, but I don't think I can help after all."

"What?"

"I don't think you'd fit in here. Good luck finding something else."

God sat up in his chair and leaned across the desk.

"Are you kidding me?"

"No, I'm afraid not."

"This is about the V8, isn't it?"

"I'm sorry, but you really should go."

"You don't understand. I can't leave without a job. It's

two days before the wedding."

"Then you don't have time to waste. Good day."

The Pope turned away and pretended to type at his computer, even though it wasn't on. God stood up and paused for a moment. He couldn't believe it. He had the job in his hands and just like that, it was gone. He looked at the Pope, who had turned away and was drinking his V8. God turned and left without another word. He wandered through the hallway with no particular destination in mind. He had no interviews the next day, no other people to ask, and no hope.

God found himself in a cafe and sat, dejected, at a table. The cafe was empty, save for God and the sole employee, who was cleaning up behind the counter. God rested his head in his hands and started to softly cry. He quickly tried to pull himself together when the employee approached him.

"Sorry," said God. "I know, you're getting ready to close. I'll be on my way."

"It's alright, we don't close for a few more minutes," said Allee´. "Are you OK?"

God shook his head.

"Not really. I'm supposed to get married in a couple of days, but I don't think it's going to happen."

"Why not?"

"Because," said God. "I can't get married without a job. I've got no prospects for one. I'm afraid the wedding is off."

Allee´ thought for a moment and regarded God carefully. He seemed like a nice guy, if a little bit on the pathetic side. She could see he'd been crying. She sighed and went behind the counter to get an application. She handed it to God.

"I've been looking for an assistant barista. You can start tomorrow if you want."

God looked up and smiled.

"Really? You mean it?"

"Yeah. Sure."

God filled out the application and handed it to Allee´. She smiled at him and shook his hand.

"Be here at 10. Wear comfortable shoes."

God practically skipped out of the cafe. He went home, as excited as a kid before Christmas that knew for sure that he was going to get a genuine Red Rider carbine air rifle with a compass in the stock and this thing that tells time.

When he got home, Sally greeted him at the door with a kiss.

"Good news," said God. "I got a job!"

Sally beamed and kissed him again.

"That's great!" she said. "What's the job?"

God looked sheepish.

"I'm an assistant barista at the Vatican coffee shop."

Sally laughed and grabbed God's arm.

"Come on now, really. What's the job?"

"No, seriously," said God. "That's the job."

Sally sobered and kissed God again.

"I'm proud of you," she said.

God smiled, almost believing her. Sally took his arm and led him to the bedroom.

"We better get to bed," said Sally. "You've got work tomorrow."

"I don't work until ten. Why do we need to go to bed now?"

Sally arched an eyebrow and put a hand on one hip.

"Oh," said God. "I get it."

God and Sally went to bed and, eventually, went to sleep.

The next day God went to his first day at work. He fidgeted with his name tag. He had never been much of a coffee drinker. In fact, he had never made coffee before in his entire life. He had thought it would be easy, but unfortunately he was a complete spaz the entire day. By the end of his shift, he still couldn't make a single drink by himself. Sure, it had only been a few hours, but still. Not even a simple cappuccino?

Allee´ approached him as God was getting ready to clock out. She leaned on the counter as God took off his apron and hung it on a hook.

"Hey," Allee´ said. "So how do you think it went?"

God wiped sweat from his brow and grimaced.

"It's a lot harder than it looks," God said. "But I'll get the hang of it."

Allee´ nodded and God clocked out for the day. He tried to put the disaster of a day behind him. He was employed and that was what counted. Sure, it was kind of humiliating to report to a teenage girl with an accent mark in her name and not even be good at the job. Just the same, it meant the wedding was on. He was glad that in a little less than 24 hours, the whole affair would be done with. He and Sally would finally be married. He hurried home, where Sally was waiting for him. She smiled as he entered the living room and sat down next to her on the couch.

"I thought you weren't going to stay here tonight. Tradition and all," he said.

"I'm not," said Sally. "But I wanted to see you after your first day. How did it go? Do you get a good discount on coffee?"

God shrugged.

"It went OK, I guess. Still getting the hang of things. And no. Ten percent."

"Don't worry, I won't ask you to make me a coffee," she said. "After all, I'll have enough trouble sleeping as it is. I can't believe we're getting married tomorrow!"

"Me either," said God. "I can't wait for it to be over."

"I don't know," said Sally. "It's been so long in coming, I'll be kind of sad when it's over. Know what I mean?"

"Not really. For me, it's been one humiliation after another. The dance lessons, all the questions you'd ask me about catering and whatnot that you completely ignored me on. Your mother. Even this job. I'm just glad to be done with it all. It can just be me and you. That's what I'm looking forward to."

God and Sally kissed and she snuggled next to him, placing her head on his shoulder. She sighed and closed her eyes.

"Yeah. After tomorrow, the only one that can humiliate you," she said. "Is me."

God smiled and stroked her hair gently. She opened her eyes and gave God another quick kiss before rising. She straightened her hair and headed towards the door.

"I guess I should go though. It may be a silly tradition, but you never want to start out on the wrong foot."

Sally left, leaving God alone with his thoughts. He wasn't getting cold feet, he was genuinely looking forward to the wedding. In fact, he didn't even really understand what getting cold feet meant. He would understand if the expression were getting hot feet. That would make some sense, because if your feet were hot, you'd be jumpy and more apt to move your feet, as if running away. Cold feet didn't make any sense. The most you would do is put on an extra pair of socks. Unless the Bible has something in it about how many pairs of socks people are permitted to wear during a wedding, God didn't see how cold feet could enter into it. Sure, maybe the Book of Ruth had something about shoes in it, but he was pretty sure socks weren't mentioned. God wasn't even sure people wore socks when the Bible was originally written. He pictured more of a sandal situation. Maybe that's why people had cold feet in the first place.

God's feet were moderate in temperature. No chance of last-minute concerns causing him to leave Sally at the altar. He was more worried that all the millions of details Sally had spent so much time deciding on would work out. Unfortunately there was little God could do to help, since he hadn't paid the slightest attention to any of those details through this point in the process. The most he could do was worry and so that is what he did.

CHAPTER FORTY-TWO: IT'S A MATTER OF DEFINITION

Tito was a little unsure about this new Cardinal the Pope had brought in, who somehow had managed to just waltz in the door and become the golden boy, next in line for Popehood. Ever since he arrived, Rowdy had involved Tito into an elaborate scheme that had something to do with God's wedding day. So far, it hadn't really amounted to much. Rowdy had created some scale drawings of the Vatican and positioned G.I. Joe figures around it to stand in for Anglican invaders, with Cobra as the Catholics. It didn't seem very realistic, either in terms of numbers or in terms of firepower. As far as he knew, he and Rowdy were the only two people involved and their combined firepower would not match Destro and Serpentor. He figured they more closely resembled the rabble of blueshirts, destined to be cannon fodder for Joe's forces. Rowdy was getting even more excited, now that the big day, as he constantly referred to it, was just hours away.

"So,' said Rowdy. "We're one day away, what do you think of the plan?"

"Honestly, I don't get it," said Tito.

"Would an interpretive dance help?"

"Uh, no."

"Good. I'm not much of a dancer. I can do a half-decent cha-cha, but that gives you a very limited vocabulary in interpretive dance. To really get anything substantive across, you need to know Baladi. Unfortunately, I was kicked out of Baladi class for extreme flatulence."

"Baladi?"

"It's a Near Eastern dance," said Rowdy. "Forget I mentioned it."

"Done. Now what?"

"Now, we wait."

"I hate waiting," Tito said, drumming his fingers on the table. "What is it we're waiting for again?"

"For the wedding."

"Yes, but why?"

"Because," said Rowdy, exasperated. "That's when the battle will happen."

Tito frowned. He didn't like the sound of that. Sure, it explained Rowdy's bizarre G.I. Joe fixation, but the prospect of an actual battle was a little much to take in. Especially a battle to happen during God's wedding. Tito wasn't sure he wanted any part of it.

"I don't want to start a battle."

"We won't be starting a battle, we'll be finishing it," Rowdy said.

"Just the same," said Tito. "It's God's wedding. It seems sacrilegious."

"I don't follow."

"He turned people into pillars of salt for looking back onto their home, for crying out loud. What's he going to do to people battling at his wedding?"

"Uh, I don't know. Tabasco sauce?"

"Tabasco sauce?"

"Yeah. It's a condiment."

"But salt isn't a condiment."

"Then what is it then?" said Rowdy.

"It's a seasoning."

"Tabasco sauce is a kind of seasoning."

"You just said it was a condiment."

"Fine, whatever, have it your way," said Rowdy. "So God won't turn you into a pile of Tabasco sauce. You win."

"A pile of Tabasco sauce?" said Tito. "How do you make a pile of Tabasco sauce? It's a liquid, for crying out loud."

"But it's God. He can do anything. He's omnipotent."

"It isn't a matter of omnipotence, it's a matter of definition. You can't have a pile of a liquid. A pool, sure. A puddle. A splash, maybe. A pond perhaps. Reservoir. But no piles."

"What if the Tabasco was frozen, like into little balls or discs or something? You could have a pile of Tabasco then."

"I suppose," said Tito. "But then it wouldn't really be a sauce anymore."

"Either way," Rowdy said. "The point is that we'll be fighting on God's side here. He might turn the other guys into a pile of Tabasco - or a puddle, if you must. But not us."

Tito sighed. He looked again at the strategically placed G.I. Joe men, the scale drawings scattered across the table. He had to admit, it seemed like a fine plan. If a battle was to be necessary, the plan seemed like it would result in victory. Of course, Tito's battle experience was limited to making the former Cardinal who was having a quasi-gay wedding the next day jump like a girl trying to recover his glasses.

"So," said Tito. "What do we do now?"

"Now we wait."

"I hate waiting."

Tito looked around and toyed with one of the G.I. Joe figures. If he remembered right, it was Lady Jaye, but it might have been Cover Girl. Either way, she would have been a compelling reason to join the military rather than the church. Oh well, there's no going back at this point, Tito was far past the maximum age for joining the military. Plus, neither Lady Jaye nor Cover Girl were really in the military, or real at all for that matter. Tito's assessment of Lady Jaye's (or Cover Girl's) recruiting ability was interrupted by the appearance of Chuck. He paused, peering at Tito and Rowdy, then continued walking toward them.

"Hey guys," Chuck said, squeezing his way past the G.I. Joe figures and the scale drawings. He knocked over Serpentor and kept walking down the hall. Rowdy glared at Chuck as he walked away.

"Thanks a lot, buddy," Rowdy said as he put Serpentor back on his feet. "No need to do anything, I got it."

Chuck disappeared down the hallway.

"Well, you really shouldn't have set all this up in the hallway," said Tito. "People are bound to walk by and knock it over. I told you, we should've set it up in my room."

Rowdy shrugged. They had gone to Tito's room, but it smelled vaguely of bacon and not in a good, "Wow, someone just made bacon" kind of way, but in a "Ew, someone left uncooked bacon sitting out for a week" kind of way. Even more distressing, the room looked fairly clean, so where the odor was coming from was a real mystery. In a way, Rowdy would have been more comfortable using Tito's room if there had been some empty pizza boxes sitting around that could potentially have accounted for the smell.

"Sorry," said Rowdy. "We should probably put this stuff away now and get some sleep. It's going to be a big day tomorrow. We need to be ready."

Tito nodded and tried not to think about the fact that he really had no idea what he was doing tomorrow. He picked up Lady Jaye (He decided it wasn't Cover Girl after all), slipped her in his pocket, and walked to his room. He locked the door, got undressed, then got into bed. He tried to sleep, but kept tossing and turning. Hours passed. Finally, he leaned out of bed and grabbed his pants from the floor. He reached into his pocket and brought Lady Jaye out. He placed her gently on his pillow and finally Tito fell asleep.

Back in his room, Chuck planned out his outfit for the wedding. He picked out a power suit and tie, classic Gordon Gekko. He considered writing out a short speech, in the event that he was asked to say something as the new god. He decided he could just wing it. Chuck had a lot of prior experience launching into impromptu soliloquies describing his grandiose visions of world domination. He didn't expect to have any trouble.

Chuck's phone rang and he answered it. An automated voice, smooth, professional, and irrepressibly cheerful, immediately began to speak:

Good evening Chuck.

We hope you are enjoying your time as god. Unfortunately you have not yet submitted the required reports. Your extended deadline expires tomorrow. Please remedy this situation promptly. Failure to do so will result in substantial sanctions.

Have a nice day!

Chuck hung up the phone. He glanced at his computer, where message after message reminding him of the daily reports waited. He yawned and rubbed his eyes. The reports could wait.

CHAPTER FORTY-THREE: THERE HE IS

The next morning, anticipation hung in the air like Denzel Washington's dialogue from the courtroom scene in *Philadelphia*. The Vatican buzzed with the last-minute duties associated with the wedding. Decorations were being placed, the cake was brought in, the faint strains of a harpist warming up floated through the Vatican's halls. Sally rushed through the morning, getting her hair done, makeup applied, and of course being strapped into her wedding dress. She also checked with the caterer, made last-minute decisions on party favors that had been lost, replacing them with bags of color-matched jelly beans. It was the best option available. It seemed like every ten seconds, someone was approaching Sally to ask a question, give her an update, or alert her to a problem. Meanwhile, God took a mid-morning nap before getting dressed.

God and the Holy Ghost stood around the chapel, waiting. They nodded to Jesus as he walked in with his date and took a seat on the groom side. God grimaced, as Jesus's date was drinking soda from a can as she chatted on her cell phone before the ceremony. Guests began filing in. God saw Johnny, with no date, walk down the aisle, notice Jesus, and take a seat a few pews away. The Cardinals, including Tito and Rowdy, sat in a single line, just behind Sally's mother in the second row. The Pope sat next to Sally's mother in the front row. She seemed visibly annoyed at the Pope's hat, which obscured her view of the proceedings. As a good Catholic, she refused to say anything about it.

At long last, the big moment arrived. The music rose and everyone stood, looking down the aisle as Sally materialized in the doorway, looking radiant, as brides always do. She smiled and began her march down the aisle toward her soon-to-be-husband. When she arrived at the altar, she handed her flowers to her mother, then turned to God, who took her hands in his. The crowd remained standing as the officiant took his position. He raised his hands and gestured for the crowd to sit.

"Ladies and gentlemen," said Pat Sajak. "We are gathered here today, to join this man and this woman in the bonds of holy matrimony."

God glanced involuntarily toward Sally's mother. She didn't appear to be trying to object, but God couldn't be certain, since the Pope's hat blocked most of her from view. Her feet, at least, had no objections. The only sound was Jesus's date finally ending her phone call after promising to call back once 'this stupid wedding' was over.

Pat smiled and spread his arms over the congregation, giving the opening blessing. During Mass, God's attention wandered. He had always found Mass excruciating, but Sally had insisted. God kept trying to sneak glances over his shoulder. He would catch Sally's glare, then revert his attention forward. Pat was really laying the Jesus angle on thick in the homily. God was sure Jesus was loving every second of it. God was beginning to regret ordaining Pat for the occasion. Finally Pat wrapped it up and went into the exchange of vows.

"The happy couple has decided to write their own

vows," said Pat. "Sally?"

Sally smiled and took God's hands in hers. She looked into his eyes and took a deep breath. Sally flicked her hair out of her eyes, took a second deep breath, and began.

"God, I love you with all my heart. Ever since we first met, you've been the most surprising, funny, and caring man I could ever hope for. I'm so glad to take you as my husband and I look forward to growing old with you."

Sally paused.

"You do grow old, right?"

God nodded and Sally sighed.

"When I went to Jamaica, I never expected to find the man of my dreams," she continued. "I'm so glad I did. I promise to love, honor, and cherish you the rest of my days, no matter what challenges those days bring. I love you."

Sally wiped tears from her eyes, with a broad smile on her face. Her hands trembled in his, as God straightened up, preparing to speak his vows. He squeezed her hands briefly and smiled.

"Sally," he said. "Ever since you fell out of that airplane and fell into my life, I've known you were the woman for me. All my life, I've needed a woman like you: One who keeps me honest, puts up with my jokes, and isn't too shabby in the looks department. In my career, I've heard millions of prayers to bring the right person into someone's life. I don't pray, but thankfully, mine was answered anyway. I love you and I promise to do my best as your husband to provide for you. I'm not wealthy, I don't have much to offer, but my love. I may not be much, but I'm all I've got. And now I'm yours forever. I love you."

God and Sally smiled at each other, as Pat stepped forward to continue the ceremony. They exchanged rings, after recovering when one of them dropped the ring. I would tell you which one, but I don't want to embarrass God unnecessarily. God and Sally faced each other again, holding each other's hands and gazing into each other's eyes. Pat raised his arm, ready to declare them husband and wife, when a muffled explosion sounded behind the altar and smoke billowed out. From within the smoke, Rasputin and Diamondhead emerged from a hole in the floor, leading to the catacombs.

"Attention, Catholics," said Rasputin. "Make no attempt to resist. Our Anglican forces have interrupted this ceremony to ensure you all may witness the greatest Anglican victory in history!"

"You are powerless to resist. Our Anglican forces - Anglican?" said Diamondhead. "I thought we worked for the Pope. So this isn't Church House after all?"

"No, of course not," said Rasputin. "This is the Vatican."

"So why am I helping you?"

"Because you're an idiot."

Diamondhead nodded.

"Ah yes. Now I remember."

It was astonishing that there wasn't mass chaos, but the wedding guests mostly just sat there, wondering what exactly was going on, thinking maybe this was something special that only happens during god weddings. Tito and Rowdy quietly made their way around the back of the altar, while Frank was frantically trying to rouse Thor, who had spent most of the ceremony sound asleep. Unfortunately Thor was a very sound sleeper. Frank was also reluctant to use much force in waking him, since Thor tended to respond to force with more force. Excessive force, usually. It was his specialty. Finally Thor roused, as Rasputin continued to ramble on about the Anglican dominance, blah, blah, blah. Thor rubbed his eyes and glared at Frank.

"What is it?" said Thor.

Frank pointed to the altar, where Diamondhead had moved to the opening in the floor, trying to help someone else through, while Rasputin waxed poetic about the glorious victory they were all about to witness. It looked to

Frank like he was stalling a little bit, he may have expected whoever was coming out of the hole to move a little faster. He was getting impatient. This gave Thor a moment to clear his head and locate Mjollnir, his hammer. He glanced at Frank.

"So, what's going on?" said Thor.

"Can't you see? The Anglicans have taken over."

"So, this isn't a usual part of a Catholic wedding?"

"No. Not at all."

"Got it. So we initiate plan A?"

"What's plan A?" said Frank. "What are you talking about?"

"Plan A: Fighting and drinking. My favorite plan of all time. I've never needed any other, in fact."

"Well, as far as drinking goes, I think all we have is communion wine. It's at the altar though, right behind them."

"Say no more. Two very unhappy Anglicans, coming up."

Thor ran up the aisle, punching an usher on the way, just to get some practice in. Rasputin saw him coming and abandoned his droning on in favor of some evasive maneuvers. He dodged Thor's initial attack. Thor stumbled on the altar and regrouped for another assault. Thor growled, ran towards Rasputin, and hit him in the head with Mjollnir. Rasputin fell back, onto the floor, either unconscious or dead. Thor turned toward Diamondhead, who was now surrounded by a half a dozen people that had emerged from the catacombs. Despite Rasputin's earlier comments, they looked less an insurmountable invading force than a lost tour group in search of a guide. Thor's intensity waned slightly, unsure of where to direct his rage. He looked for Frank for assistance, but Frank was still trying to make his way up the aisle, his reluctance to punch perfect strangers in the face causing it to take a great deal longer than it had for Thor.

Thor turned back to Diamondhead, who now had a dozen or so people around him, still none looking that threatening, except for one guy who looked eerily like Vincent Price. Still, he wasn't exactly threatening, but creepy. Thor hesitated and in that brief moment, Rasputin climbed onto his back, trying to choke him unconscious. Thor threw himself backward, but they were in the middle of the room, no walls around for Thor to try to slam Rasputin into. Thor flailed about, trying to throw Rasputin off his back, but Rasputin had a surprisingly good grip for someone who seemed to have passed on to that great Anglican mass in the sky only moments before. Thor fell to his knees, weakening under Rasputin's grip. He was about to pass out, when Frank emerged from the aisle and stabbed Rasputin in the back. Rasputin's grip slackened and he fell from Thor's back.

Thor breathed deeply, rubbing his neck as he tried to reorient himself. Rasputin was trying to remove the knife from his back, as Frank backed away. Frank wasn't much of a fighter. He had assumed Thor would do the heavy lifting in that category. God had taken Sally away from the melee, where Pat sat calmly.

"Can't you do something?" said Sally. "They are ruining our wedding."

"What can I do?" said Pat. "I just give people money for spinning a large, colorful wheel and having basic spelling skills. I think they need to work things out for themselves."

"Not you," said Sally. "Him."

Sally jerked her finger toward God, who looked surprised. He glanced around, just in case there was someone behind him that might be better suited to deal with the problem, like Michael Westen from *Burn Notice*. That's a good show, if you've never seen it. It's on Netflix, but don't start watching it if you don't have some extra time, because once you start, you'll soon be watching three or four episodes a day. Seriously. But there was no Michael

Westen standing behind God. Sally meant him after all.

"What do you expect me to do?" said God. "I don't even reward mediocre spelling skills."

"You're God, you've got to be able to do something."

"I'm retired," God muttered under his breath, surveying the scene. He didn't want any part of Rasputin, that's for sure. He was still recovering from the knife wound, but he still looked tougher and more ill-tempered than God wanted to deal with. God decided to check out what was going on with the growing group of people stationed just inside the chapel, having emerged from the hole Rasputin had created. God walked over cautiously. They didn't look dangerous, most of them just looked confused. God looked at the first one, that had initially appeared with Rasputin.

"Hey, man, how's it going?" said God.

"Fine, fine," said Diamondhead. "No complaints. How are things with you?"

"Could be better, I'm glad you asked," said God. "You see, I'm in the middle of my wedding and all this ruckus is causing my wife-to-be quite a bit of distress. Do you think you could see your way to corralling that friend of yours and taking your tour group here somewhere else for a few hours?"

God smiled and Diamondhead smiled back. God nodded and Diamondhead nodded back. God chuckled nervously and Diamondhead chuckled back. God's smiled disappeared and he looked intently at Diamondhead.

"So, you'll get out of here then?"

"What?" said Diamondhead. "Me?"

"Yes, you. You're interrupting my wedding."

"And you would prefer that I didn't?"

"Yes."

"Are you quite sure? I was getting the impression that you really wanted us to interrupt, so that you didn't really have to get married after all."

"No. I am quite content with getting married, I would

really appreciate it if you all would clear out."

"I would like to, really," said Diamondhead. "But I'm not really the one in charge. You see, that over there is Wolfgang Amadeus Groenemeyer. He has no cousins."

Diamondhead pointed to Rasputin. God looked at Rasputin, then back at Diamondhead, then back at Rasputin. He didn't see the connection. He looked back at Diamondhead.

"I don't care how many cousins he has," said God. "You need to get him out of here."

"But he's the boss, you see."

"Because he doesn't have any cousins?"

"No."

"Then why?"

"Well, he's Anglican and I'm an idiot."

"I see that. What's his being Anglican have to do with anything?"

"The Anglicans have raised the dead, in order to crush the Catholic church once and for all. Or so I gather."

"Raised the dead? What dead?"

"These dead."

Diamondhead gestured to the dozens of people standing around. God looked and they seemed perfectly normal people, aside from the one guy who looked exactly like Vincent Price. Many of them were dressed in clothes that were marginally out of date. God would have realized that they were more our of date than he thought, but his fashion sense was stuck in 1980's era beachwear, so in comparison some of them looked positively fashionable. God tapped one of them on the shoulder.

"Hi, sorry to trouble you," God said. "But my friend here would have me believe that you have just risen from the dead. Is that true?"

"I don't know," said the man. "The last thing I remember, I was in a hospital. Then I woke up here."

"So why are you working with the Anglicans?"

"What Anglicans?"

"These two," said God, pointing to Diamondhead and Rasputin. "Wolfgang Amadeus Groenemeyer over there and this guy."

"My name is Diamondhead," said Diamondhead. "But I'm not an Anglican. Just an idiot. As I said."

"Is there really a difference?"

Diamondhead shrugged.

"I'm not working with the Anglicans," the resurrected man said. "Whoever they are. I'm Catholic."

"Yeah," said Diamondhead. "I think Rasputin was imagining more of a *Night of the Living Dead* scenario."

God questioned some of the others and they were all Catholic, all had no ill intent, and all had no idea how they had gotten there.

"Well, you all are welcome to stay for the rest of the ceremony," God said. "If you could just take your seats."

The group milled around for a second, then started filing down the aisle. God went back to Sally as the group disbanded. Rasputin, now back on his feet, glared at the people filing into the pews.

"What are you doing?" he shrieked. "Attack the Catholics! Attack!"

The man who had been talking to God turned to look at Rasputin.

"Look, Wolfgang," said the man. "We are Catholic."

The man turned his back on Rasputin and took his seat. Rasputin fumed to himself. He couldn't believe that now, after all this time, Diamondhead had finally remembered their code names. The fact that the Anglican's entire plan was backfiring was truly a secondary annoyance. He glanced around and saw Thor had also recovered, ready for round two. The rest of the room was strangely silent, as the crowd waited in anticipation of what Rasputin might do next.

Rasputin turned to Thor and shouted. It was not English, but an inchoate scream that announced to everyone present that plans be damned, but Rasputin was

Eric M. Ralph

not going to give up without a fight. Even though there had already been a fight, Rasputin was not going to give up without a longer, more drawn-out fight. Sure, he had been beaten and stabbed, but it was nothing he hadn't been through before. He ran at Thor, who ducked, and dove at Rasputin's legs, causing him to collapse on top of Thor. The two wrestled back and forth, until Rasputin grabbed a vase and raised it above his head, intending to smash it over Thor's head. As he did, a shot rang out. A bullet hole appeared in Rasputin's chest. He dropped the vase and put a hand over the wound. He gazed at the blood pouring out, in shock. He looked up to see Diamondhead put his gun back in his coat. Rasputin's mouth fell open and he fell sideways onto the floor.

Thor got up and dusted himself off. He looked at Rasputin, then looked at Diamondhead.

"Thanks," he said. "But I had it under control."

"Sure," said Diamondhead. "I know you did. I just figured I'd, you know, hurry it along a little bit."

Thor nodded and approached that thing on the altar that holds the holy water, which is called an aspersorium. Go ahead and impress people at the office by working that into conversation tomorrow. It's the bowl, not the shaker thing, which is called an aspergillum, in case you were wondering. Thor was about to sprinkle some water on his face, to refresh himself a little bit, when he heard a collective gasp from the crowd. He turned around and saw Rasputin, again on his feet, looking very tired and very angry. Clearly he did not appreciate being hit with a hammer, stabbed, and shot. Rasputin lunged toward Thor, who parried his attacks, took Rasputin by the back of his head, and shoved his face into the aspersorium. He held Rasputin underwater, until finally Rasputin's body went limp. Thor removed him from the aspersorium and threw his body down at the base of the altar. Thor stumbled towards the pews, where he fell into an empty seat.

"Sure are a lot of freaks running around the Vatican,"

said Thor as he lay down in the front pew to pass out cold.

Rowdy and Tito had lingered in the back throughout the battle, waiting for the key moment. The moment had arrived and they emerged from the shadows. Now that Rasputin's plan had collapsed like a soufflé taken out of the oven too soon, they were primed to take action. Rowdy stepped forward.

"People of the Vatican," said Rowdy. "Now that we are rid of that ridiculous plan, I will activate the real Anglican plan. First, take a look at this!"

Rowdy took out the formerly really cool-looking thing. Somehow, in the middle of the Vatican chapel, with Rasputin's body lying on the floor, Thor passed out in a pew, and with God and Pat Sajak standing there, it didn't seem so cool any more. Rowdy shook it in anger and threw it away.

"OK, how about this?"

Rowdy took out his Thermos and spilled beef vegetable soup onto the floor. The crowd stood silent, feeling somewhat embarrassed on Rowdy's behalf.

"Fine," said Rowdy, growing increasingly desperate. "Tito, give the signal. Anglicans, show yourselves and rid us of the Catholic scourge!"

The Catholics looked around expectantly, searching for any sign of the impending invasion by the mighty Anglican army. Nothing seemed to be happening.

God coughed quietly and it echoed throughout the room.

Rowdy looked around the room, then turned to look at Tito.

"Didn't you call them?"

"Who?"

"The Anglican army. They are supposed to be here."

"The Anglicans have an army? And I was supposed to call them?"

"Yes, of course. What did you think those G.I. Joes figures were all about?"

"I had no idea. I didn't even realize we were working for the Anglicans. I thought you were positioning yourself to be the next Pope. I'm a Cardinal, for crying out loud. What made you believe I was working for the Anglicans?"

"Well, you gave the countersign."

"Countersign?"

"Yes, I asked how your day was going and you said, 'Fine, thanks. And you?' That's the countersign."

"Don't Anglicans normally say 'fine' when asked how they are?"

"Yes, but we don't inquire about others. It's considered impolite to pry."

Rowdy surveyed the crowd once more.

"So, I'm guessing that a Cobra-style army is not going to invade any second."

"No. I wouldn't think so."

"Ah. That changes things then. Simpler, I suppose, but not as exciting. I was looking forward to seeing the flame throwers and such. Maybe someone on a snowmobile, possibly holding a crossbow. A hot chick dressed in all black, maybe with a whip. Oh well."

Rowdy shrugged his shoulders and looked lost for a moment. Then his face brightened.

"Just kidding everyone," he said. "I'm really a Catholic, just pulling your legs."

He looked at the Pope in the front row.

"We're cool, right?"

Rowdy raised his hand, in anticipation of a high-five. The Pope just stared.

"Don't leave me hanging."

The Pope reluctantly high-fived Rowdy, who smiled.

"Great," said Rowdy. He leaned in towards the Pope.

"I'm still open to being the next Pope, by the way."

Louder, he said to the crowd, "Well, back to the main event, I suppose. Pat?"

Pat Sajak stepped over Rasputin's prone form, back onto the altar, and God and Sally followed. Rowdy and

Tito took their seats with the other Cardinals. Pat raised his arms over the couple.

"As I was saying," said Pat. "With the power vested in me by God, the Vatican, and the country of Jamaica, I now declare you husband and wife. You may kiss the bride."

God tried going in for the kiss, but Rasputin was in the way. Sally kicked him off the altar and he fell with a thud in the front row. Unhampered, God went in for the kiss. It was a good one. Once they came up for air, they turned to the crowd, who cheered wildly. Pat smiled, the music rose, and God and Sally walked back down the aisle as the crowd roared.

CHAPTER FORTY-FOUR: SLIGHTLY UNCOMFORTABLE

When God and Sally reached the door, they saw a man waiting outside, looking depressed. God was about to walk by, but something made him pause. Sally looked at the man and approached him.

"Are you OK?" she asked.

The man looked up, with tears in his eyes.

"Yeah, I'm OK, I guess," said 'Bud.'

"Come on now," said Sally. "Why are you crying?"

"It's my wedding. Or it isn't my wedding."

"What do you mean?"

"I'm supposed to get married in a few minutes, but we can't find an officiant."

"Why not?"

"Well," said 'Bud.' "We're not a normal couple. We're...unconventional."

God snapped his fingers and pointed at 'Bud.'

"You're the quasi-gay wedding, aren't you?"

"Yeah," said 'Bud.' "But there's not really anything quasi about it, really. It's just gay. Or would be, if it were actually going to happen. It doesn't matter, I guess, since no one was coming anyway."

God looked at Sally, then whispered in her ear. She smiled and nodded.

"I could officiate," God said. "How does that sound?"

'Bud' smiled, but the tears continued. He couldn't manage any words, but nodded enthusiastically. He wiped the tears from his eyes.

"Great," God said. "Now I'm driving the bus!"

"What?" said Bud. "What bus?"

"It's my catchphrase."

"Don't pay any attention to him," said Sally. "I told you a million times, God, that is never going to catch on."

God went back inside to tell everyone to hang out for awhile since they'd be having another wedding. Outside, 'Bud' chatted with Sally.

"So is he really able to marry us?" said 'Bud.'

"Yeah," said Sally. "He's God, so I think you're good on that score."

"He's God? So who are you?"

"I'm his wife."

"His wife?"

"Yep, we just got married. If you think your wedding will be unconventional, you should have seen ours. A guy got drowned in the holy water bucket."

"Really?"

"Yeah. Technically I suppose it wasn't part of the ceremony, but it happened. Some Anglican nut tried to take over. Very strange. It's all better now though."

"I'm glad it worked out," said 'Bud.' "I better let my fiancé know that we're on after all."

'Bud' ran off to tell Buddy and soon the two of them were at the altar, the chapel filled with guests, and God in front of them to officiate the ceremony. Bud and Buddy were both dressed in tuxedos and held each other's hands as they gazed into each other's eyes. God smiled and began the ceremony.

"Friends, we are gathered here to join this man and, uh,

this other man," said God. "In the bonds of holy matrimony. Anyone got a problem with that?"

God looked around and the crowd gave a collective shrug.

"Sorry if I'm a little informal," said God to Bud and Buddy. "But I've never done this before. Plus formality isn't really in my nature."

"It's not a problem," said Buddy. "We're not formal either."

"Good." God smiled again and tried to remember where he'd left off.

"So no objections. Perfect. Bud, do you want Buddy to be your husband, for better or worse, as long as you both live, even if he turns out to have a lot of annoying habits that you never realized he had until you started living together?"

"I do," said Bud.

"I wanted to use these vows at my own wedding," said God. "But I was overruled. I'm not sure which of you will have to get used to being overruled, but to whoever it is, good luck. Buddy, same question to you, with the names appropriately switched. You ready to spend your life with this guy?"

"Absolutely."

"Fantastic. You guys have rings?"

Bud and Buddy handed God the rings.

"Thanks. The rings are like true love, no beginning and no end. Also like the movie Lost Highway, for similar reasons. Watch it sometime and you'll see what I mean. OK, I forget what exactly gets said here, but give each other your rings."

Bud gave Buddy his ring and vice-versa.

"OK, by the power vested in me, by, uh, me," God said. "I pronounce you husband and husband. What I've put together, let no man put asunder."

God leaned in conspiratorially.

"That's always been my favorite line."

God stood straight up and looked toward Sally and Pat. "Pat, you forgot the put asunder part."

"Sorry, God," said Pat. "But I was a little stressed, seeing as there had been a pitch battle between good and evil just before that part."

"Good and evil," said God. "Ha. Just some Anglicans and a Scandinavian. No offense, Thor."

Thor nodded cheerfully, having located the communion wine shortly after he had woken up from his battle with Rasputin.

"I'm sorry, guys," said God. "I got distracted. OK, no one can put you asunder. You may kiss the husband."

Bud and Buddy kissed and it made a large part of the crowd fairly uncomfortable, even though they knew it shouldn't and they did their best to hide it. Thankfully, it was short and tasteful. The happy couple turned to walk back down the aisle and the crowd gave a heartfelt cheer.

CHAPTER FORTY-FIVE: BETTER LATE THAN NEVER

As they neared the exit, 'Bud' and Buddy paused. The sky had gone dark and a low groan rumbled from the ground beneath them. The Vatican began to shake and the crowd started to panic. Shrieks rose from the crowd. God drew Sally close to him. 'Bud' and Buddy took shelter as best they could behind the pews. Thor, Frank, and Pat Sajak huddled together, gazing up at the sky and wondering what was going on. The recently rejuvenated dead started to reconsider their luck.

"What's happening?" shouted Sally over the din.

God shrugged, the only response possible as the roof exploded outward and wind swept through the building. God protected Sally with his arms, trying to withstand the gale forces that whined in their ears. Within the confusion, God heard a guttural growl. Sally shrieked in terror as a monstrous abomination waddled down the aisle, straight toward the newlyweds. God smiled and tried in vain to extend his hand as Sally clutched him tightly.

"Trall!" God shouted. "It's good to see you. I'm glad you could make it."

Trall produced another set of grotesque sounds in response.

"It's been a little rocky, so far," said God. "Do you know what's going on?"

The winds surged, nearly blowing God and Sally to the ground and drowning out Trall's response. God held onto Sally tightly, waiting for the winds to subside. Sally began to sob in fear. God tightened his grip on her, bracing himself against the swirling winds that seemed to scream through the room. During a brief respite, God leaned in closer to Trall, struggling to make out the creature's rumbling speech. God's face darkened as he realized what Trall was saying. He took Sally back to where Thor, Pat, and Frank sat in wonder. God placed Sally into Thor's arms.

"Take care of her," he shouted.

Sally protested, but God shook his head.

"I think I can stop this," God said. "Don't worry. It'll all be OK."

He winked at Sally, then turned to the crowd. In the darkness, the wind swirling and carrying debris through the air, God had trouble seeing. He peered into the shadows until he saw a familiar large hat. God struggled against the wind until he was at the Pope's side.

"Where's Chuck?" said God.

"Who?"

"Chuck. The new god. You know. Your Lord and Savior. Chuck, damn it, Chuck!"

"Oh," said the Pope. "That Chuck."

The Pope craned his neck, scanning what was left of the pews. Another tremor shook the floors and the Pope fell to his knees. His eyes widened. The Pope pointed to the back of the church.

"There," said the Pope. "In the dark grey suit, grey tie. Greased-back hair."

God squinted through the gloom.

"You mean the one that looks like a Mafia wanna-be?"

The Pope nodded. God grimaced and stormed his way to where Chuck cowered in the last pew. God surged toward Chuck, grabbing him by the lapels and screaming into his face.

"The reports! Why didn't you file the reports?"

A sudden lapse in the winds caused the word 'reports' to echo through the room. Chuck whimpered and cowered, shrinking into his power suit. God punched him in the face and Chuck fell to the ground. Chuck's phone clattered to the floor. God picked it up and it buzzed in his hands.

"I'll check it," said God. "It might be important."

God looked contemptuously down at Chuck, who groaned.

"You hit me," whined Chuck.

God ignored him. He fumbled with the phone, but was able to access Chuck's emails. Message after message alerted them to what God already knew - Chuck was woefully deficient in his reporting. God frowned at the phone.

"I only wish I knew how to work these things," said God. "It took me long enough to submit the reports on computer. This thing doesn't even have a keyboard."

God fell to one knee as the ground again trembled, with a massive groan the floor ruptured, separating the front from the back by a widening chasm. He steadied himself with the pew until the rumbling stopped. A loud hiss erupted from the rift in the floor. Steam poured from the gap.

"Uh-oh," said God, peering into the void. "We've got a problem."

"What is it now?" said Chuck.

"Lava, it looks like. It's rising up the crevasse. We've got five minutes, maybe, until we're going to have to either find somewhere else to stand, or learn to be fireproof."

The wind picked up again, howling through what was left of the room. God put his hands to his mouth and shouted as loud as he could.

"Does anyone know anything about submitting reports?"

Frank's ears perked up. He raised his hand.

"I do," said Frank. "I'm an accountant."

"Get to work then. You've got five minutes. Catch."

God cocked his arm and threw a perfect pass to Frank. The phone glanced off of Frank's fingers and onto the floor. God winced, hoping no damage was done. He glanced back into the pit of rising lava.

"Now you've got four minutes."

Frank grabbed the phone and his fingers flew over the screen. The virtual keyboard clacked away incessantly, as one message then another disappeared from the screen as the reports were submitted. Frank paused for a second to wipe sweat from his brow. A clap of thunder roared through the room and hail poured from the sky. Frank ducked underneath the altar. Pat Sajak used his jacket to protect Frank from the hail as best he could. The wind shrieked, lightening crashed around them, setting fire to the remaining walls. Smoke billowed from the walls, causing Frank to sputter and choke. Pat wrapped his tie around Frank's face to help him breathe. All the while Frank's fingers continued their work, a seeming blur speeding around the phone. God watched the rising lava and urged Frank on under his breath.

"Come on, we don't have all day. You can do it."

There was no hope of Frank hearing God's encouragement over the roar of the wind, the pounding of the hail, the whistle of the steam, and the reverberation of the earth. God watched as Frank continued to work. Frank stopped typing and let out a sigh. He tossed the phone back to God.

"Done!" Frank yelled.

Frank pumped his fist in celebration and raised both arms to the sky. God smiled but his good mood was short-lived. The wind continued to roar, the hail continued to pound, the steam continued to boil, and the ground continued to tremble.

"What's the problem?" Frank shouted. "Why didn't it stop?"

God shook his head and looked at the phone. The phone buzzed with a new message.

Greetings Chuck.

Thank you for submitting your reports. Unfortunately we cannot accept reports submitted on your behalf without your approval. Please approve your reports as soon as possible. In the meantime, the apocalypse will continue. Please be sure to bring in any outdoor pets. Have a nice day!

God turned to locate Chuck. He was cringing beneath the pew, only his feet sticking out. God grabbed his feet and yanked him out. Chuck hid behind his arms, shielding himself from God's gaze. God forced his arms down and pushed the phone into his hands.

Behind them the crevasse was nearly filled with boiling lava. God pulled at his collar and wiped sweat from his forehead. The heat was unimaginable.

"Approve the reports, Chuck," God screamed.

God raised his fist, ready to beat Chuck senseless until the reports were approved. Chuck took a deep breath and focused on the phone, hitting keys expertly. He exhaled as he hit 'Send.'

The wind wound down and the trembling stopped. The hail lightened, then shifted to a warm rain, which extinguished the flames still smoldering at what remained of the Vatican walls. The clouds broke slightly, allowing sun to stream down on the crowd, who was gradually emerging from the shelter they had sought. The lava cooled and receded back into the depths. The hole remained, splitting the Vatican in two.

Pope John Paul Georgianringo emerged from the rubble, rubbing his forehead as he surveyed the damage. He shook his head and a wry smile appeared on his face.

"Damn," he said. "I guess those idiots that warned me

against allowing gay marriage were right after all. Who would have thought it?'"

CHAPTER FORTY-SIX: FIRST VAN HALEN, NOW THIS

God led the crowd across the street to Giovanni's, which had been blessedly spared from the destruction. The Pope hat that had blown onto the roof was the only sign that anything awry had transpired.

God, Sally, Bud, and Buddy all sat at the head table during dinner. God really enjoyed himself and as a side benefit, people were more reluctant to do the 'clink the glasses to make the couple kiss' routine when Bud and Buddy kissed as well. God was especially glad that the ceremony had gone off without a hitch. Sure, it had been interrupted by an attempted Anglican invasion and a near-apocalyptic event, but the important thing was that it went off without a hitch that Sally could have blamed God for.

Sally's mother had even given her blessing, even though she was less than impressed with God's new job. Everyone was also too polite to point out that God's new workplace was now buried under the smoldering rubble that had once been the Vatican.

After cutting the cake, God and Sally sat looking at each other, rapt. They finished their cake and were enjoying a cup of coffee when Jesus walked up. He slapped God on the back as they shook hands.

"Congrats, man," said Jesus. "You've got quite a lady there."

"I sure do. You've got quite the lady too."

God gestured towards Jesus's date, who was grinding on Cardinal Tito out on the dance floor as the DJ played "Sexy And I Know It."

"Yeah, Starla is something special alright. I was thinking though, that maybe I've been kind of a jerk lately and that maybe we could get Trinity back together."

God's jaw slackened in surprise and he furrowed his brow.

"Well…"

"Well what?" said Jesus. "I'm not usually one to apologize, it took a lot for me to ask you guys to take me back. What's the problem?"

"It's just that, uh," said God. "We already hired David Lee Roth to replace you."

This time it was Jesus that was surprised. He scowled, glanced over his shoulder, and put his finger in God's chest.

"You think that washed-up, second-rate, no-talent clown can replace me? What a joke. Trinity is dead. You hear me? Dead."

Jesus turned to leave, but God caught him by the shoulder to stop him.

"Hold on," said God. "Calm down. Have a drink. I'll talk to the Holy Ghost about it and see if we can let Roth down easy. We didn't think you were coming back, so thought we'd move on."

God stuck out his hand and Jesus reluctantly shook it. Jesus turned away and made his way to the dance floor, where he pushed Cardinal Tito out of the way to dance with Starla. She barely noticed, only temporarily suspending her grinding as she switched from Tito to Jesus. Sally looked on and shook her head.

"I don't think she's wearing underwear," said Sally.

God shook his head and made a concerted effort not to look over toward the dance floor. He squeezed Sally's hand and leaned in for a brief kiss.

"Please," he said. "Do not make me imagine Starla without underwear."

"I'm telling you," said Sally. "There's no need to imagine. That woman is not wearing underwear."

"Can't we talk about something else?"

"I'm just saying."

"Well, can you just not say? This is after all our first real conversation as a married couple."

"OK, good point. Let's talk about something else."

"Actually, let's not talk," said God. "Let's dance."

God took Sally by the hand and led her to the dance floor. He signaled to the DJ, who announced that the bride and groom would be dancing their first dance. The two danced and God acquitted himself nicely. Chaz would have been proud, had he not been committed to a mental institution following God's final lesson.

After the dance, they kissed and walked back to the head table, where the Pope stood with a microphone in his hand. The Pope blew into the microphone and started tapping it with his hand.

"Is this thing on?"

'Yes,' the crowd moaned.

"Is this thing on?"

The crowd groaned again and God assured the Pope that the microphone was, in fact, on. The Pope stood behind God and Sally, and looked into the crowd.

"I know the best man usually does the toast," said the Pope. "But God didn't have one, so I figured I would step up to the plate. First off, I'd like to congratulate God on a great choice of wife. I always figured that he would end up with a fatty boombalatty, but Sally is far from it. Not like that girl I took to the prom. Bitch took all my money and went off to Chicago. I couldn't believe it. Of course, she's dead now. I also want to commend them on a wonderful wedding. At first I thought it was going to be the same old thing, but then you added in that fake Anglican invasion, it really spiced things up quite nicely, so well done there. If the Vatican ever gets rebuilt, you are more than welcome to marry there again, once you divorce each other and find someone else half your age. Let's all raise a glass."

The Pope picked up his V8 and raised it in the air.

"To Sally and God: May you forever be happy, healthy, and free of green beans."

The Pope downed the V8 and the crowd started to clap, but the Pope picked up the microphone again and continued.

"Now I'd like to ask for a moment of silence in the memory of Michael Jackson."

The Pope bowed his head and the crowd followed suit. The Pope grabbed the bridge of his nose and strained to hold back tears. After a moment, the sound of the Pope softly sobbing reverberated through the microphone. The Pope wiped away his tears with his sleeve and put the microphone down before moving back to his seat, where Cardinal Jermaine comforted him.

Thor and Frank sat at the bar, taking in the whole scene. Frank couldn't quite believe that he was actually a guest at God's wedding reception. The food hadn't been as good as he would have expected from God's reception, but a slightly overcooked chicken couldn't take the shine off of the experience for Frank. Thor, on the other hand, was still recovering from the action during the ceremony and was slightly miffed that the bartender didn't have his favorite drink on hand. That didn't stop him from drinking truly impressive amounts of beer, but still. It was the principle of the matter.

Frank turned around in his seat, facing the head table. Thor signaled the bartender for another beer. Frank rubbed his hands on his pants and took a deep breath. He glanced over at Thor.

"This is it, this is really it," said Frank.

"This is what?"

"This is when I finally get to meet God."

"I really don't see the big deal," said Thor. "He's a nice guy and all, but I don't get all the fuss you make about meeting him."

"Well, it's a big deal for me. Where I come from, you don't get to meet gods every day."

"You've been with a god every day for the last month or two though."

"Yeah," said Frank. "No offense, but, it's not the same. If I'd grown up in Scandinavia worshipping you, then yes, it would be amazing to have met you. I'm still glad to have met you, but it isn't the same as meeting the God I grew up with."

Thor shrugged.

"No one in Scandinavia worships me anymore either," he said. "The most respect I get these days is from Marvel Comics fanboys. They think of me as a comic superhero, not really a god at all. Plus that ridiculous hat they have me wearing in the comics; it's embarrassing. I might as well be Aquaman."

Frank put his hand on Thor's shoulder.

"You might not have my worship," said Frank. "But you have my respect. Plus they still teach courses about you in college. Aquaman can't say that. Except at Michigan State and that hardly counts."

Thor smiled briefly, then took another drink of beer.

"Thanks, Frank, that means a lot. Now get over there and meet God. You've certainly earned it."

Frank hopped down from his bar stool and rubbed his hand together. He nodded toward Thor, then made his way over to where God and Sally were talking. God smiled at Frank as he approached.

"Hey," said God. "I've been meaning to thank you for all your help during the ceremony. And, you know, saving us all from the apocalypse."

God stood up and shook Frank's hand as Frank stood, frozen in space. God smiled again, then gestured to the table.

"Have a seat."

Frank silently sat, still tongue-tied. God gestured toward Sally.

"This is my wife, Sally," he said.

Frank looked toward Sally and finally unfroze. He reached out and shook her hand.

"Frank," he said. "I'm so glad to meet you both."

"It's our pleasure," said Sally. "Without you and Thor, who knows what would have happened?"

Frank glanced downward. He hadn't expected praise.

"It's nothing," said Frank. "I just filed some reports and Thor loves to fight. It's what we do, I guess."

"In any case, we appreciate it," said God. "How do you know Thor?"

"I met him looking for you."

"Looking for me?"

"Yeah," said Frank. "You visited me once, by accident. I've been looking for you ever since."

"I visited you?"

"Yeah, you were trying to find Pat Sajak. Right before you retired, as I understand it. You were in the form of a dog and came barking outside my door."

"I'm certainly glad I did. Otherwise the ceremony would have been a complete disaster."

Frank stood up and looked toward the bar.

"I should get going," said Frank. "If Thor drinks alone for too long, something bad is bound to happen. Besides, I really just wanted to meet you. Not for any real reason, I guess. Sounds a little nutty when I say it like that."

God shrugged.

"Not really," said God. "Lots of people wanted to meet me, you know, without dying. It was my pleasure though. Here's my pager number. Give me a call, maybe we all could go to dinner or something."

Frank took God's card and looked it thoughtfully. He nodded as he turned to leave. He walked slowly back to the bar, where Thor was still drinking. Thor smiled as he saw Frank reappear.

"How did it go?" said Thor.

Frank shrugged.

"Fine. Nice guy."

"Was it all you'd hoped?"

"I don't know," said Frank. "I'm not really sure what I was hoping for. He was very appreciative of you putting the smack down on the Anglicans."

"Did he really say that? He said 'putting the smack down'?"

"No, but he was definitely thankful."

"Did he give you any cash?"

"Cash? Why would he give me cash?"

"Cash is an expression of gratitude. The best expression of gratitude, in fact."

Frank grimaced, turned to the bartender, and ordered himself a drink. He was about to castigate Thor, at least, as much as anyone can castigate Thor, for Thor's comment about cash being an expression of gratitude, but was interrupted by Pat Sajak leaning in between them to get himself a mojito.

"Hey," said Frank. "Nice job with the ceremony."

"Thanks," said Pat. "You guys did a nice job with dispatching the Anglicans."

"Thanks."

"Mind if I have a seat?"

Pat pulled up a stool and sat between the two of them. He sipped his mojito, demonstrating perfect artfulness and precision in drinking and tasting every flavor, every molecule of the mojito as it passed down his throat. Frank felt like he could taste the mojito just by watching Pat drink it. Pat put the glass down, looked at Frank, looked at Thor, then turned towards the dance floor. Frank looked at the dance floor as well and glanced sidelong at Pat.

"So, Pat," said Frank. "What's it all mean?"

Pat smiled inwardly and outwardly.

"It's all a Devil's Haircut, my friend."

"What? How so?"

"None of it makes any sense, but it sure was fun at the time."

"Is that what that song means?" said Thor. "I've always wondered."

EPILOGUE: THE FITZ-HUME
DEFENSE

The Pope grimaced, glaring across the table at the Archbishop of Canterbury. The Pope had just lost Missoula, Montana. He rose from the table and went to pour himself a glass of water. He drank the water and the cold of the water helped him refocus. The negotiations were going poorly for the Catholics. In addition to losing Missoula, they had already lost Liechtenstein, most of Tallahassee, and everyone in Luxembourg except Tatiana Fabeck. The only places the Catholics had won so far were Delft (in the Netherlands) and Hoboken, New Jersey. The Pope returned to the table, sat down, and took a fresh look at things.

The Pope considered changing his strategy. He had selected 'rock' every time so far, under the theory that the Archbishop would have to choose something other than paper sooner or later. Besides, how in the hell does paper beat a rock anyway? So paper covers rock. So what? What the hell does the rock care? Using that logic, blankets would beat mattresses, but you don't see anyone playing Pillow-Blanket-Mattress. In any realistic scenario, rock beats paper. People have been known to use rocks as paperweights, after all. No one has ever covered a rock with paper in real life. The Pope decided to give 'rock' one more shot.

"One, two, three, shoot!"

The Pope threw out rock and the Archbishop covered with paper. Walla Walla, Washington was now another Anglican stronghold. The Pope cursed his luck and turned to Cardinal Tito.

"You take over," said the Pope. "He's in my head. He's got some sort of hex on me, it's like he knows what I'm going to throw before I do. He must be using the Milbarge technique."

Tito nodded and took the Pope's seat across from the Archbishop. The Pope tried to remember why they had selected Paper-Rock-Scissors as the way to settle the dispute. Other suggestions had been made, but somehow Hungry Hungry Hippos hadn't seemed like an appropriately dignified way to decide the religious fate of everyone in the world. In the Christian world anyway.

The Pope pinched the bridge of his nose, a pulsing headache had come on, as if it were punishing him for losing Walla Walla. The Pope couldn't help thinking: Was this all really necessary? Did they really need to go city-by-city, playing a kids' game for each metropolitan area? And how did Tatiana Fabeck manage to get special treatment? Couldn't they have just let things be after the Beck reference and have foregone all this nonsense? What really was the point of it all?

The Pope sat next to Agent Rowdy, who was once again carrying a He-Man Thermos, a pen, a bottle of common household cleanser, and the thing that everyone had once thought so cool. He had thrown the 'Transubstantiation is NOT Bull' button away, since its purpose had been served.

"Why do you still carry that thing around?" said the Pope. "It's no longer cool, you know."

"I know," said Rowdy. "But I'm hoping it'll soon make it to kitsch, then to retro, at which point I'll be able to sell it to a hipster."

"A hipster?"

"Sure, hipsters love stuff that is kitschy-retro-cool."

"But how can you sell it? You don't even know what it is."

"Good point. Maybe it has a name or something written on it somewhere that would give us a clue, or at least help us describe it on Craigslist."

"Craigslist? Not eBay?"

"Hipsters don't use eBay."

"They don't?"

"No."

"Why not?" said the Pope.

"Because eBay hasn't been cool for years."

"But having your kidney stolen by some faker on Craigslist is cool?"

"That's just an urban legend."

"No it isn't. It happened to a friend of mine."

"Yeah? Who?"

"Well, it was more of a friend of a friend. I think his name was Steve."

"Who was this Steve a friend of?"

"I don't remember."

"Uh-huh."

Rowdy fiddled with the formerly cool thing, looking for anything that might suggest what it was, what it did, or who made it. On the bottom, just underneath what seemed to be a battery cover for impossibly large batteries. The little diagram called for size Q. Rowdy saw a single word, printed in barely raised black type against the black body of the item: Sampo.

"Wow, a Sampo," said Rowdy. "Guess I owe that guy an apology."

"Just think about how Martha Rae must feel. To have her underwear drawer violated for nothing like that."

"How did you know about that?"

"I follow her on Twitter."

"Twitter. Ugh," said Rowdy. "I quit Twitter after I accidentally incurred the wrath of all the Depeche Mode fans on Twitter by saying that I was kind of sick of all the 'Personal Jesus' remixes. I mean, I like the song, but to have an entire album of remixes of the same song? Get real."

"Depeche Mode has a lot of fans on Twitter?"

"Apparently. Don't get them angry, believe me."

"After all this, would you still be interested in being the next Pope?"

"Me? You do realize I was working for the Anglicans, right?"

The Pope shrugged.

"Nobody's perfect."

Rowdy smiled.

"Sure, I guess. I don't really have anything better to do. The Anglicans aren't even paying me to be a spy anymore."

"It's funny, I said the same thing when they asked me to be the Pope."

"Are there any other loose ends we need to tie up first?"

"Not that I can think of. Besides, anything left has to be pretty minute. We even tied up that Sampo thing, for crying out loud."

"Yeah, but you know fans. They'll be on the Internet instantly after they're done reading, logging their displeasure at any part of it not tied up into a neat little package."

"Eh," said the Pope. "We'll just tell them it'll be addressed in the sequel."

"There's going to be a sequel?"

ABOUT THE AUTHOR

Eric M. Ralph was born in Toledo, Ohio. He graduated from St. Francis de Sales high school before attending the Ohio State University and earning a bachelor's degree in finance and his MBA. Eric has a black belt in Kenpo karate, a DTM from Toastmasters International, and plays third trombone in a community orchestra.

Find Eric at ericmralph.com, on Google+, or on Twitter @eric_ralph

www.ingramcontent.com/pod-product-compliance
Lightning Source LLC
Chambersburg PA
CBHW060741050426
42449CB00008B/1285